MY POCKET
mantras

POWERFUL WORDS TO
CONNECT, COMFORT, AND PROTECT

TANAAZ CHUBB

ADAMS MEDIA
NEW YORK   LONDON   TORONTO   SYDNEY   NEW DELHI

Adams Media
An Imprint of Simon & Schuster, Inc.
57 Littlefield Street
Avon, Massachusetts 02322

First Adams Media trade paperback edition MARCH 2018

ADAMS MEDIA and colophon are trademarks of Simon and Schuster.

For information about special discounts for bulk purchases, please contact Simon & Schuster Special Sales at 1-866-506-1949 or business@simonandschuster.com.

The Simon & Schuster Speakers Bureau can bring authors to your live event. For more information or to book an event contact the Simon & Schuster Speakers Bureau at 1-866-248-3049 or visit our website at www.simonspeakers.com.

Interior design by Katrina Machado
Interior images © iStockphoto.com/hpkalyani

Manufactured in China

10 9 8 7 6

Library of Congress Cataloging-in-Publication Data has been applied for.

ISBN 978-1-5072-0578-5
ISBN 978-1-5072-0579-2 (ebook)

CONTENTS

INTRODUCTION

A mantra is a simple phrase or sentence you can recite to yourself to improve your well-being. Whenever you need an instant pick-me-up, a boost of self-love, or simply some assistance in falling asleep, there is a mantra in this book that is the perfect fit for you. *My Pocket Mantras* is filled with 150 positive, inspiring, and healing mantras that are designed to help lift your spirits, heal your heart, and brighten your day as you navigate through all of life's ups and downs.

All of these mantras are written from the heart and are designed to help you shift your mindset, release stress, enhance your inner connection—and, in time, even change your life. You might find yourself letting go of past hurts; feeling brighter about your future; and discovering love, peace, and balance in your life.

Simply skim through the different chapters within this book or flip to a random page and you might just find the perfect mantra to work with. Each mantra comes with instructions on how to recite it, the perfect number of times to recite it, and some insight into the intention behind the words. Try to recite the mantra daily for at least thirty days in order to experience the most benefits—however, you will probably start to experience the positive effects of reciting your mantra almost immediately.

The mantras are designed to be simple and memorable so you can recite them with ease. For best results, recite your mantra slowly and try to put a lot of belief and feeling behind the words as you say them. If you take your time and allow yourself to really feel and believe what you are saying, the mantra will have a stronger impact on your life. For some mantras, it may take time before you can really believe or feel the power behind them, but with regular practice it will become much easier. In fact, the mantras that you struggle with or resist believing are the ones you probably need to work on the most!

All the mantras contained within this book are also designed to be flexible. Feel free to adapt or edit any mantra to suit your personal or specific needs. As you get comfortable with reciting the mantras in this book, you can even experiment with writing your own.

Even though each mantra comes with instructions, it is important to remember that there really are no rules. Use your own intuition to guide you, and work with your chosen mantra in whatever way feels right for you. You may also find it beneficial to keep a written copy of the mantra in an easy-to-read place, such as above your desk, in your car, or in the bathroom. This will serve as a great reminder for you to say your mantra regularly, which will allow it to really work its magic in your life.

If you are ready to enhance your life, develop a deeper spiritual connection with yourself, and boost your feelings of positivity, *My Pocket Mantras* is just what you need.

PART 1

THE BASICS OF MANTRAS

THE AMAZING POWER OF WORDS

Words not only hold meaning, but they also hold their own special kind of magic. Words allow us to connect with others, share stories, and understand the world around us. We all know the famous magic word, *abracadabra,* but did you know that one translation of this word is "I create as I speak"? Words have the ability to shift your mindset, change your perception, and even create the world that you live in.

Humans have long understood the power of words, not just for communication but also for healing purposes. Words turn into wishes, prayers, and beliefs that can help healing. Words carry their own vibrations, and these vibrations can create a ripple effect in the Universe. This ripple effect can influence your mood, your mind, and your life.

You may have already experienced these effects in your own life and observed how words or thoughts have influenced your attitudes, feelings, and actions. You experience a situation very differently, for example, when someone says something mean and nasty to you versus when someone says something loving and kind to you.

WHAT IS A MANTRA?

Mantras are short, rhythmic statements that use positive and uplifting words to create a positive and uplifting mindset. Mantras have been used for centuries across various religions and cultures to help individuals set intentions about what they want to create in their lives and to bring about healing and spiritual enlightenment. Reciting mantras might have been the first type of meditation practice. Today, mantras are also used in yoga and other healing practices.

Mantras come in many forms and are found in many different languages, but all of them serve to heal and raise spiritual awareness. The word *mantra* can be loosely translated to "instrument of the mind." Mantras can be used as instruments to free your mind from stresses, doubts, and fears and replace them with positive, inspired, and action-driven thoughts.

THE BENEFITS OF MANTRAS

The vibration that a mantra creates can change how you perceive your reality, shift your mindset, and create new, positive beliefs about yourself. Even if you don't initially believe or feel the words of a mantra wholeheartedly, simply reciting it regularly can help your brain rewire your beliefs and change the way you view yourself.

In order for mantras to be effective, they need to be said with a strong intention and a powerful feeling behind them. This is done to enhance the vibrational quality of the mantra and to accelerate its healing effects in your life. Mantras can work on physical, mental/emotional, and spiritual levels.

Physical
On a physical level, reciting mantras has been shown to:
* Boost your concentration and focus
* Lower your heart rate and blood pressure

According to traditional Chinese medicine, mantras can also stimulate the endocrine system, bringing balance to the body.

Mental/Emotional
On a mental or emotional level, reciting mantras can:
* Help relieve feelings of stress and anxiety
* Teach you how to love and find compassion for yourself
* Give you the strength and inspiration to lead a positive, purposeful, and joyous life no matter what the circumstances

Spiritual
On a spiritual level, reciting mantras can help to:
* Release bad karma
* Increase spiritual enlightenment and wisdom
* Stimulate the energy centers (chakras) in your mouth and throat so you can better express yourself

HOW OFTEN SHOULD YOU RECITE A MANTRA?

In traditional practices, mantras must be recited 125,000 times in order to be effective. It is believed that after this many repetitions, the vibration can infuse the mantra into your heart, bringing you a new awareness. But don't worry; simply chanting the mantra daily as frequently as possible and with as much belief as possible can be just as effective.

Throughout the book, you will see instructions for reciting a mantra a particular number of times. These recommended repetition counts are based on the minimum amount of times you will need to recite the mantra in order to have it begin to seep into the depths of your mind. However, everyone is going to feel things differently, so be sure to use your own intuition or judgment when it comes to how many repetitions are right for you. Often the mantras that you need the most in your life are the hardest to say and need the most repetitions before you really start to "feel" them on the deepest of levels. When you have reached the perfect repetition count, you should begin to feel a shift in your mindset.

MANTRAS: SIMPLE WORDS THAT CAN CHANGE YOUR LIFE!

By investing just a few minutes each day, you will be able to experience the many benefits that mantras can bring into your life. Why not give them a try and see how they can make your life's journey a happier and healthier one?

PART 2

THE MANTRAS

CHAPTER 1

MANTRAS TO START THE DAY

These mantras are designed to give you a boost of inspiration first thing in the morning so you can start the day off on the right foot and with a pep in your step. Use these mantras to increase your energy and enthusiasm so that you can thrive in the day ahead.

TODAY WILL BE A WONDERFUL DAY, FILLED WITH MANY BLESSINGS.

How and when to recite this mantra: Recite this mantra three times either out loud or quietly to yourself as soon as you wake up. For best results, reach your arms up high, look to the sky, and take a big stretch as you say these words. This stretch will also invigorate your entire body and get you energized for the day ahead.

How this mantra can help you: If you long to start your day off feeling excited and anticipating the many blessings that await you, this is the perfect mantra for you. This mantra will not only boost your mood, but it will also allow you to shift your awareness so that you will notice all the positive things that come your way through the day, no matter how small they may be. Stating that your day will be wonderful helps you recognize all the things that are going right in your life and prevents you from getting bogged down in the things that are perhaps not going so well. This shift in awareness will increase your feelings of positivity and excitement and will give you a more solution-based outlook. This mantra also encourages feelings of gratitude, helping you feel more aware of the many blessings that surround you.

I HAVE SO MUCH TO LOOK FORWARD TO TODAY.

How and when to recite this mantra: Recite this mantra three times either out loud or quietly to yourself as soon as you wake up. For added effect, keep repeating this mantra until you are actually up and out of bed.

How this mantra can help you: Do you struggle to get out of bed each morning? This mantra helps motivate you for the day ahead and gets you looking forward to the day rather than dreading it. Even if you don't feel like you have anything to look forward to, simply stating the words can help you shift your mindset so you feel more excited and motivated by your day-to-day life. In truth, you probably always have *something* to look forward to, and by reciting this mantra, you give yourself room to slowly start to list those things on a daily basis. From finding pleasure in a delicious breakfast to reading a good book on your train ride to work, or simply hanging out with loved ones, life is always giving you something you can cherish and something you can look forward to. Through reciting this mantra and paying attention to the many blessings that surround you, you will soon start seeing a myriad of things to look forward to every single day.

JOY SURROUNDS ME EVERYWHERE I GO.

How and when to recite this mantra: Recite this mantra three times either out loud or quietly to yourself first thing in the morning. Try to smile as you say it. You can also use this mantra later in the day if you need an instant energy boost.

How this mantra can help you: Imagine if everywhere you went, a trail of joyful, abundant, and positive energy followed you. Reciting this mantra helps you create the vibration of joy in all areas of your life. In fact, by working with this mantra regularly, you can soon start to feel that joy is following you everywhere!

In the short term, this mantra is designed to help evoke feelings of lightheartedness and positivity as you move through the day. In the long term, this mantra can give you the ability to spread the energy and vibration of joy to all areas of your life, and even to others. Think of this mantra like a boost of good vibes that can rub off on everyone you meet. This mantra is also great to use when you find yourself dealing with negative or draining situations. By reciting the mantra during times like these, you can bring out feelings of joy, positivity, and confidence. This, in turn, will help you tackle problems head-on without feeling negative or devoid of energy.

TODAY I CAN RELAX, AS ALL MY NEEDS ARE BEING TAKEN CARE OF.

How and when to recite this mantra: Recite this mantra five times either out loud or quietly to yourself first thing in the morning. Breathe in and out deeply after you say it. This mantra is perfect to recite if you are feeling particularly overwhelmed or stressed about your day ahead. You can also use it during the day if you start to feel anxious or when overwhelming thoughts creep in.

How this mantra can help you: What would it feel like to completely trust and surrender to your life? Many people constantly feel the need to control things, and as a result they are often stressed or anxious. Life can sometimes feel overwhelming, but if you are able to let go of your worries, things have a funny way of working themselves out. Sometimes the situations and problems in your life don't need your constant involvement. If you take a step back and look at things from afar, your perspective might change significantly.

This mantra helps to encapsulate this feeling, and it is a strong reminder that you don't have to do everything or have everything figured out all at once. Give yourself permission to relax, surrender, and let life take its natural course. This mantra will also help you build trust in the Universe and believe that everything will work out in its own time and as it needs to.

I AM STRONG ENOUGH TO HANDLE WHATEVER COMES MY WAY.

How and when to recite this mantra: Recite this mantra three times either out loud or quietly to yourself first thing in the morning.

How this mantra can help you: This mantra reminds you that you have the strength and power to get through whatever obstacles, challenges, or opportunities come your way. Remember, you are a strong, powerful human being with the potential to do and achieve anything! Reciting this mantra as you start your day will put you in a confident and positive frame of mind that will empower you to keep pushing through difficult situations. It will also encourage you to persist in times of adversity and will help you open up your mind to potential solutions. When you have a positive "can do" mindset, there is truly nothing you can't handle, and this mantra will definitely remind you of that. Over time, this mantra will naturally help you to boost your feelings of self-confidence and self-esteem so you always feel prepared to tackle all of life's ups and downs, no matter how challenging they may appear.

TODAY I FEEL ENERGIZED AND INVIGORATED BY LIFE.

How and when to recite this mantra: State this mantra three times aloud or silently to yourself while lightly jumping or jogging in one spot. The movement will boost your energy levels and instantly invigorate you. This is also a great mantra to recite during your morning workout.

How this mantra can help you: Many of us need a boost of energy first thing in the morning. Instead of turning to copious amounts of coffee, try using this mantra instead. By chanting these words, you will feel inspired to tackle the day ahead and be motivated to accomplish whatever tasks need to be dealt with. Energizing your body with these words also grants you more stamina to get through the day and helps you to tackle head-on any issues that arise.

This mantra is also great to use when you find yourself feeling bored or despondent about your life. At times we can all get stuck in a rut; it's understandable. Reciting this mantra regularly will help you feel invigorated and passionate about life so that you can pursue all of your goals and dreams. In time, this mantra will also naturally boost your energy levels and help you to create a new zest and attitude for life.

I EMBRACE WHATEVER THE DAY BRINGS. I KNOW I AM PROTECTED.

How and when to recite this mantra: Recite this mantra quietly to yourself seven times first thing in the morning with your hands in a prayer position. This mantra can be particularly helpful when you are in an uncertain period of your life or when you are anticipating that a challenging situation may arise during the day.

How this mantra can help you: Life is always dishing out things that are not part of your plan, but even when this happens it is important to remember that you are always going to be protected by the amazing, supportive forces of the Universe. As long as you truly believe and trust that you are being protected and cared for, you will see examples of this protection in your life.

This mantra is designed to help you accept and embrace whatever comes your way while also offering hope. Even though it can be challenging to embrace difficult situations when they arise, it is actually even more challenging to resist them. Reciting this mantra will help you move through the acceptance process and will evoke feelings of support and protection. From this place, it will be a lot easier for you to navigate through your day.

THANK YOU FOR THIS BEAUTIFUL DAY. I FEEL GRATEFUL TO BE ALIVE.

How and when to recite this mantra: Recite this mantra three times out loud or quietly to yourself first thing in the morning. You may want to get in the habit of saying this mantra as soon as you begin to feel yourself waking up, before you're fully awake. When you are still in this sleep state, the mantra has the ability to deeply permeate your subconscious, making it more powerful.

How this mantra can help you: This mantra instantly puts you in a positive mood and shifts your awareness into a place of gratitude. When you start to tune into feelings of gratitude, it instantly raises your energetic vibration and puts you in a positive and loving frame of mind. Feeling thankful to be alive also inspires you to make the most of every moment and every opportunity. Waking up each day is truly a gift, and acknowledging this can help you to appreciate life on a whole new level.

You have probably heard the saying, "Don't forget to stop and smell the roses." This mantra, like the saying, can help you remember to bring your awareness to all the beauty that surrounds you as you move through the day. Reciting this mantra in the morning will help you program your mind and expand your awareness so you don't miss all the small, yet beautiful, moments of life. Over time, saying this mantra can help you live life to the fullest and inspire you to take action so that you can do all the things you have always wanted to do.

TODAY I WILL FOCUS ON ALL THAT IS GOOD.

How and when to recite this mantra: Recite this mantra three to five times quietly to yourself first thing in the morning. For added benefits, as you repeat the mantra try to visualize in your mind something that makes you feel good, such as beautiful scenery from nature, a particular animal, a loved one, and so on.

How this mantra can help you: This mantra is designed to change your outlook on life by shifting your focus to all the loving, positive qualities of yourself and the world around you. All too often, we get so caught up in all the things that are going wrong in our lives that we forget about all the amazing, positive, and wonderful things that are also happening! It is very easy to zero in on the drama of a negative situation or experience, but sometimes focusing on the good things instead can help you feel more empowered. When you focus on all that is good, it can inspire you to make effective changes and come up with positive solutions to your problems. You'll also discover more happiness and enjoy life so much more. Over time, this mantra will help you to see the good in almost any situation or event that arises. There is always a silver lining, and by regularly chanting this mantra, it will become easier and easier for you to see it.

LIFE SUPPORTS ME IN MIRACULOUS WAYS.

How and when to recite this mantra: Recite this mantra while standing nine times out loud or quietly to yourself first thing in the morning. As you repeat the mantra, feel the weight of your body being supported by all of your muscles and bones. Feel the weight of your body being supported by the ground beneath you. Acknowledge that no matter what, Mother Earth will always be supporting you with the ground beneath your feet.

How this mantra can help you: Do you truly feel supported by life? This mantra is designed to help you boost your feelings of hope, faith, and positivity. When it doesn't seem like life is being supportive, it is often because you are not able to see the bigger picture. Sometimes in hindsight we are able to see that the most challenging of situations in our lives were actually the most rewarding and fulfilling. It may help to even look back at a challenging situation in your life that you've overcome. Reflect on how it made you stronger and got you to where you are today. This mantra reminds you that life is always supportive and that things will always make sense in the end. You may not always be able to understand what life sends your way, but in time things always have a way of working out.

Reciting this mantra allows you to feel supported in times of need and helps to promote positive emotions. By starting your day with this mantra, you will be guided to focus on feelings that support you in life. This simple shift in awareness can have a profound effect on your life and can fill your day with lots of positivity and happiness.

TODAY I WILL INSPIRE AND UPLIFT OTHERS.

How and when to recite this mantra: Recite this mantra as many times as needed first thing in the morning when you know you'll be interacting with lots of other people during the day. You can also use this mantra throughout the day as needed.

How this mantra can help you: Being of service to others benefits you just as much as the other people. Sometimes inspiring other people sends waves of inspiration your way. This mantra is a great one to use when you need to support and be there for others. It is also great to use when collaborating with people on important projects or when you are at work. Sometimes taking the focus off yourself and putting it onto others can be a great relief to you. Doing so can even provide you with a distraction from the things that are going on in your own life. Being of service to people can be extremely rewarding and can even help you put your own life in perspective at times. The great thing about this mantra is that by stating your intention to inspire and uplift others, you also help to inspire and uplift yourself in turn.

I RELAX AND SURRENDER TO THE FLOW OF LIFE.

How and when to recite this mantra: Recite this mantra three to four times either out loud or quietly to yourself first thing in the morning. With each repetition, reach your arms up and circle them over the top of your head. This will help to get your energy flowing and can also be very relaxing.

How this mantra can help you: Imagine how it would feel to simply relax into each day and not have to stress and worry about every little thing. Life is so much easier when we relax and surrender to its flow rather than trying to fight against it. This mantra is designed to help evoke feelings of calmness, peace, and serenity so you can begin your day from a relaxed state of mind. If you suffer from worry or stress or feel overwhelmed by the many events of the day, this mantra can help you to release the need to control everything. It will encourage mindfulness and the importance of being present. Being present throughout the day is a great way to combat stress and helps you keep focused on what is happening in the here and now. In fact, one of the main causes of stress and anxiety is dwelling on the past or thinking too far ahead in the future. When you reside in the present, life feels far more manageable and much more under control. By practicing this mantra in the morning, you can set yourself on the right course for the day ahead so that you can relax and trust wherever events may lead you.

I KNOW TODAY WILL BRING MANY MIRACLES.

How and when to recite this mantra: Recite this mantra three times out loud first thing in the morning.

How this mantra can help you: This mantra is designed to open your awareness to miracles! Miracles big and small are happening all around you every single day—the key is to notice them. It is a miracle that the sun rises each day, and it is a miracle that you can walk, talk, breathe, and move around. It truly is a miracle to be alive, and this mantra will help remind you of this as you get prepared for the day ahead. This mantra is also an excellent reminder that things are always changing for the better and that no matter what the circumstances are, miracles are always a possibility. If there is a situation in your life that needs a miracle, this mantra will open you up to finding one as long as you believe it is possible.

I AM EXCITED BY THE OPPORTUNITIES TODAY WILL BRING.

How and when to recite this mantra: Recite this mantra five times either out loud or quietly to yourself first thing in the morning. Try using it as a motivational mantra to help you get up and out of bed.

How this mantra can help you: Every day holds thousands of glittering opportunities that are just waiting for you. You just have to go out and grab them! This mantra is designed to evoke feelings of excitement about the day ahead and to open up your awareness to the many opportunities that are out there. Sometimes it is easy to get stuck in the monotony of everyday life and ignore the daily opportunities around you, such as the chance to say hi to a stranger you meet at the bus stop, or the chance to speak up when your boss asks if anyone has any inspired ideas. This mantra is highly motivational. Not only does it program you to take notice of opportunities, but it can help you act on them. It can also expand your mind so that you start to find inspiration everywhere. Over time, this mantra will help you to feel that each day holds a new chance to do something exciting and different.

TODAY I WILL TAKE STEPS IN THE DIRECTION OF MY DREAMS.

How and when to recite this mantra: Recite this mantra five times either out loud or quietly to yourself as you are getting ready for the day ahead.

How this mantra can help you: If you have a specific goal in mind—no matter how far-fetched it seems—this is the perfect mantra to use. This mantra is designed to help you find the inspiration, energy, and motivation to go after your goals, dreams, and wishes. Reciting this mantra each day brings you a daily dose of inspiration to actually take steps that are going to help you achieve all that you desire. It may take some time to get started at first, but this mantra is eventually going to help you believe in yourself more so that you can gain the confidence you need to make things happen.

This mantra also helps you become aware of the smaller and more manageable steps that you can take every day in the direction of your dreams. Sometimes it is easy to discount the smaller actions, but it's the little steps that add up to big results. In addition, going after your goals is often more about the journey than the end result, so it is important to enjoy the process and work toward making achievements every single day.

I FEEL AWAKE AND READY TO START THE DAY.

How and when to recite this mantra: Recite this mantra ten times either out loud or quietly to yourself first thing in the morning. This mantra is especially great to use when you are in a sleep-deprived state or when you are feeling apprehensive about your day for some reason. It is also perfect to use throughout the day when you need a boost of energy or an afternoon pick-me-up. For added benefits, stretch your arms up to the sky and take deep breaths while reciting this mantra.

How this mantra can help you: We all have mornings when we wake up feeling tired and struggle to get out of bed. If this resonates with you, use this mantra. It is designed to evoke feelings of alertness, energy, and inspiration so you can get the boost you need to start your day. Even if you wake up feeling groggy, reciting this mantra can actually trick your brain into feeling the opposite so you instead feel alert and energized. The more you say this mantra and bring meaning to it, the more awake and alert you are going to feel. The mind is a powerful thing, and it is amazing just how quickly this mantra can boost your energy levels and inspire feelings of alertness.

I TRUST THAT EVERYTHING IS GOING TO WORK OUT PERFECTLY.

How and when to recite this mantra: Recite this mantra three times either out loud or quietly to yourself first thing in the morning. You can also use this mantra during the day if you encounter a sticky situation.

How this mantra can help you: Starting your day off with this mantra allows you to relax and feel reassured that everything is on schedule and that everything is going to go smoothly. This doesn't necessarily mean that things are going to work exactly the way you want them to, but it does that things are going to work out as they need to and in their own time. It is important to remember that this is how life works. When you trust in life and the Universe around you, it becomes a lot easier to accept this, and it becomes a lot easier to go with the flow.

This mantra is also great to use when you are feeling overwhelmed or stressed about the events you have scheduled for the day. Reciting this mantra first thing in the morning allows you to release any fearful or worrisome thoughts (for example, a big deadline or a project at work that you're not sure you can do well) and replaces them with feelings of positivity, motivation, and a "can do" attitude.

TODAY I WILL HAVE FAITH AND ACCEPT WHAT IS.

How and when to recite this mantra: Recite this mantra three times either out loud or quietly to yourself as you get ready for the day ahead.

How this mantra can help you: Many of us move through life with expectations. We expect things to go a certain way, we expect people to understand us, and we expect certain events or situations to unfold the way we anticipate. But imagine completely surrendering, allowing life to take you wherever it wants to go; imagine freeing yourself to embrace whatever comes, as if you chose it. Life rarely goes as expected, and this mantra is designed to help you find appreciation in that. It is a perfect mantra to use if you are feeling disappointed by recent events or if you want to remain open and free of judgments or expectations.

Using this mantra, over time, helps you relax into the flow of your life, no matter how difficult or challenging things may get. Often when you release expectations and accept things just the way they are, life becomes a lot less stressful and far more enjoyable. This is not to say that you shouldn't ever imagine the future, but sometimes getting too attached to ideas and outcomes can cause unnecessary stress. Reciting this mantra will help you take a far more relaxed and simplified approach to your life, which in turn will lead you to feel more accepting and hopeful about whatever comes your way.

I KNOW I AM LOVED AND SUPPORTED AS I MOVE THROUGH THE DAY.

How and when to recite this mantra: Recite this mantra three times either out loud or quietly to yourself first thing in the morning or whenever needed. As you recite the mantra, cross your arms and wrap them around your body like you are giving yourself a big, supportive hug.

How this mantra can help you: This mantra provides instant support and comfort, and reassures you that you are not alone on this earthly journey. When you tune in, it is easy to see that you are supported by the Universe, by Mother Earth, and by the world around you. Simply taking a walk in nature and observing the ground beneath your feet—how it holds you and supports your entire body weight—is enough to help you understand how this Universe is always protecting you. As you practice this mantra, you may even start to notice more loving thoughts or experiences greeting you throughout the day.

It is also important to remember, however, that feeling loved and supported is not so much about having people around you cheering you on, but is about having more of an internal feeling, a connection with your greater environment that makes you feel like you are part of something bigger than just yourself. This higher feeling of connection is where this mantra will lead you in time. Keep saying the words over and over, especially first thing in the morning, and see how it shifts your mindset and allows you to feel forever loved.

WHATEVER I DO TODAY WILL BE ENOUGH.

How and when to recite this mantra: Recite this mantra as many times as needed either out loud or quietly to yourself in the morning. As you repeat the mantra, gently nod your head like you are saying "yes." This positive movement will help you affirm that whatever you accomplish today will indeed be enough.

How this mantra can help you: There are only so many hours in a day, and this mantra is there to help relieve any pressure you may be feeling about getting things done. Sometimes before you have even started your day, you can feel overwhelmed about all the things you need to do and all the places you need to be. This feeling can instantly make you stressed and anxious, and these draining emotions can follow you around for the rest of the day. Besides doing practical things like making a to-do list, reciting this mantra can definitely help turn an overwhelming day into a more manageable day. This mantra instantly brings acceptance and reaffirms that even though you may not get it all done, it will be okay and there will be a solution.

This mantra also serves as a reminder to be gentle with yourself and that you don't have to pressure yourself into trying to be a super-hero. There is only so much one person can get done in a day, and sometimes certain things are just going to have to wait. This mantra reminds you of that from a supportive and loving place, which in turn will help you feel less stressed and overwhelmed about the day ahead.

CHAPTER 2

MANTRAS FOR RELIEVING STRESS AND ANXIETY

Many of us live with near-constant stress and anxiety. Yet these conditions are meant to be temporary—just to help you address a specific situation. Then your body should return to its normal resting state. Constant stress puts undue strain on body and mind, in the form of headaches and stomachaches, high blood pressure, and insomnia. These mantras are designed to help bring you back to feelings of calm, peace, and ease so you can be free from the destructive results of stress and anxiety. Use these mantras whenever you need to feel protected, supported, and comforted.

I AM SAFE; ALL IS WELL.

How and when to recite this mantra: Recite this mantra three times either out loud or quietly to yourself. As you say the words, take three to five deep breaths, in and out, and visualize a golden-white light around your body, which will comfort and protect you.

How this mantra can help you: This mantra is extremely powerful and can instantly calm and relax your mind. It is designed to bring comfort and reassurance while also reducing feelings of anxiety and stress about a particular outcome or the future. It is common to feel fearful at times, but reminding yourself that you are safe and that everything is well can sometimes stop fear in its tracks. You can reprogram your fearful thoughts and replace them with positive thoughts by using this mantra. Then it becomes easier to tackle problems head-on and even face your fears.

You can also use this mantra during periods of emotional or physical illness. Reciting the words will help program your mind so that you emphasize all the aspects of your health that are going well. When you are suffering from an illness of any kind, it is very difficult not to think about it or draw attention to it. But if you shift your awareness to all the things that are going well, you can completely change your outlook and bring yourself peace of mind.

WITH EVERY BREATH, I FEEL MYSELF RELAXING.

How and when to recite this mantra: State the mantra in your mind as you inhale, and then once the mantra is complete, exhale. For added benefits, as you exhale, visualize any tension you have melting away with the breath. Repeat this three times.

How this mantra can help you: Your breath is an extremely powerful tool that can instantly evoke feelings of relaxation. This mantra is perfect to use when you need to release pent-up tension. You can use it while meditating or even when doing your daily chores. Even though stress is something you feel on an emotional level, it can impact your body as well. Over time, stress and tension can build up in your shoulders, neck, and stomach and make you feel as if you are tied in knots. When you feel tense, it reflects in your attitude and can make it very difficult to let go, relax, and surrender to the flow of life.

This mantra will help to relieve any physical or emotional tension you may be feeling as a result of extreme stress, and it can also help you to get "out of your mind." What does that mean? Very often it is your overactive mind or thoughts that make you feel stressed and anxious, but by focusing on the words and on your breath as you chant this mantra, you can give your mind a much-needed rest.

I AM STRONG ENOUGH TO GET THROUGH THIS.

How and when to recite this mantra: Recite this mantra three times out loud while standing in as straight and strong a posture as you can.

How this mantra can help you: Do you believe that you are strong enough to get through whatever life brings you? Do you believe you are strong enough to get through this current period of your life? You are. This mantra helps you realize your strength and intelligence when things may not be going as smoothly as you would like. If you are going through a rough patch, this mantra can help remind you of your strength and your ability to get through things. There is nothing that you can't handle, and this mantra is there to remind you that all you need to do is believe it and know that it is true.

This mantra also boosts your confidence and your feelings of self-esteem so you feel empowered to keep moving rather than feeling stuck. If you keep using this mantra, eventually all of your problems will feel much more manageable and, therefore, will be much easier for you to solve. You may also feel more confident in your approach to life and more assured that you have the knowledge and belief to navigate past any obstacles in your way. You are strong enough to get through whatever life brings; all you need to do is believe it and own it.

I RELAX KNOWING THAT EVERYTHING IS GOING TO BE OKAY.

How and when to recite this mantra: Recite this mantra three times either out loud or quietly to yourself whenever you are feeling stressed or anxious about a current or upcoming situation.

How this mantra can help you: Need to soothe your anxious mind? This mantra is perfect for relieving stress and anxiety, especially when you are uncertain of what the future is going to bring. This mantra has an instant calming effect and can make you feel comforted and assured about the future, no matter what it may hold for you. Along with reciting this mantra, shifting your awareness to the present moment can help you release any anxious feelings and can get you focused on what is in your control right now. This can help you approach things one step at a time, which removes the stress of needing to have everything figured out.

This mantra is also extremely supportive and serves as a reminder that no matter what happens, you are going to be okay. We often need to remind ourselves of this, especially when anxiety or stress kicks in.

I KNOW THAT THE PERFECT SOLUTION IS ON THE WAY.

How and when to recite this mantra: When you are looking for clarity or reassurance on the path ahead, recite this mantra three times out loud or quietly to yourself.

How this mantra can help you: This mantra is perfect to use when you are feeling unsure of how to proceed. When you feel confused about which path to take, often it is because you need to wait for more information to be revealed. Eventually, things will start to make sense, but reaching this stage can sometimes require a lot of patience!

Confusion can also be a sign that growth and change are in the works—and those are positive things in the long run. Perhaps not knowing where to go next is a sign that you need to rest and take some time out to get clearer about your life ahead. To fast-track the process and to reach a feeling of clarity quicker, use this mantra. It instantly switches your mindset so that you focus on solutions and what you do know, rather than getting caught up in uncertainty. This mantra is also designed to make you more responsive to the perfect solution when it does arrive and can open you up to the many subtle clues that the Universe can sometimes leave for you. The Universe is always providing assistance for you along your life journey, so pay attention to synchronicities, signs, and your gut feelings.

I HAVE CONTROL OVER HOW I FEEL, AND I CHOOSE TO FEEL AT PEACE.

How and when to recite this mantra: For best results, place your hand over your heart as you recite these words three times out loud or to yourself. This will help to instill peace in your heart and your body.

How this mantra can help you: This mantra is very powerful and helps to remind you that you may not be in control of everything in life, but that you are in control of how you feel. In fact, the only thing that you really have control over is how you respond to the situations that come your way. Your thoughts are often responsible for dictating how you feel, and if you learn to manage your thoughts, in turn you can also learn to manage your feelings. You can manage your thoughts by allowing yourself to recognize them, then encouraging yourself to let go of them. Experiencing and then releasing your thoughts is a healthy way of processing what you're going through without getting stuck.

While expressing your feelings is important, this mantra also allows you to feel in control and calm and balanced when your emotions start to feel out of control. We all go through times in our lives when stress or anxiety can get the better of us, but this mantra reminds us to operate from a place of peace instead. This mantra is also perfect to use when you are feeling overwhelmed emotionally and are unsure of how to deal with whatever life has thrown your way. If you are still struggling with uncontrollable emotions, physical exercise can be a great way to let off excess steam. Simply taking a brisk walk in nature can be extremely therapeutic.

I HAVE SO MUCH TO BE THANKFUL FOR.

How and when to recite this mantra: Recite this mantra three to five times out loud, then list a few things that come to mind that you are currently grateful for.

How this mantra can help you: It is extremely important to regularly honor all the things you have to be thankful for. This mantra will shift your awareness from a place of stress and anxiety and into a place of gratitude. Focusing on the things that you have to be thankful for can instantly lift your spirits and boost your mood. In fact, feeling thankful is one of the most powerful energetic vibrations in the Universe, and feeling it regularly can bring about amazing life changes. Encouraging yourself to list a few things that you feel grateful for after reciting this mantra will keep the momentum going after you say the words.

This mantra can also help you shift your focus away from any stressful or anxious thoughts and onto thoughts that make you feel strong and empowered. Feeling thankful is an extremely powerful emotion that can help you embrace all the positive things in your life.

THIS TOO SHALL PASS.

How and when to recite this mantra: Recite this mantra seven times out loud or quietly to yourself during challenging life periods and when you are working through painful emotions.

How this mantra can help you: This powerful Zen mantra is extremely effective and serves as a reminder that everything in life is temporary. Life ebbs and flows and things come and go, which means that you shouldn't get attached to things. When you become attached to material things or outcomes, that is when you can create disappointment and suffering for yourself. When you remember that life is transient and that everything is always shifting and changing, then you can feel more comfortable and more at peace when life brings events your way that are uncomfortable. Stating this mantra instantly brings comfort and assures you that nothing will last forever. Whatever is stirring for you in your life, either internally or externally, will pass. Eventually it will be nothing but a distant memory. Eventually you will heal, you will move on, and things will be different. If you are dealing with a challenging situation, this mantra can bring you a sense of peace from within, no matter how chaotic things are on the outside.

LIFE IS ALWAYS SUPPORTING ME THROUGH THE TWISTS AND TURNS.

How and when to recite this mantra: Recite this mantra three times either out loud or quietly to yourself when you are feeling overwhelmed or stressed by recent events.

How this mantra can help you: This mantra acknowledges and brings acceptance to the fact that life is rarely a smooth journey. Life is instead studded with surprising twists and turns that always seem to keep us growing, learning, and evolving. Life really is a series of ups and downs, and the more we can expect this and understand this, the more we can relax and enjoy the flow of life. In fact, the more we can accept this, the more we can start to see life as an adventure that we don't need to take so seriously. While life is valuable, taking it too seriously leads to feelings of stress and burnout. Instead, if you bring some lightness and fun into your life, things will feel so much easier.

This mantra is also perfect to use when you feel overwhelmed or are surrounded by chaos. By reciting this mantra as instructed, it can help you restore faith, peace, and harmony in your body. It also helps you accept whatever is surrounding you and whatever is waiting around the corner. Reciting this mantra will open your awareness to just how supportive life can be.

ALL EXPERIENCES ARE HELPING ME GROW.

How and when to recite this mantra: Recite this mantra four times either out loud or quietly to yourself as often as needed.

How this mantra can help you: This mantra is perfect to use when you are searching for answers to challenges that have come your way. Life is a journey of growth, and by acknowledging this, you can see the higher purpose in everything that happens. It may not always be easy to see exactly how you'll grow from a particular situation, but understanding that all experiences are contributing to your growth and development can be reassuring and can help you tackle things from a place of curiosity rather than despair.

Viewing all experiences as opportunities to grow allows you to focus on the bigger picture and helps you avoid getting caught up in all the details. You'll be able to take a step back and not put so much pressure on yourself to have everything figured out. You are here to learn, and part of that process requires you to go through experiences that are indeed challenging and confusing—but also ultimately joyful. The more you can approach life as a learning experience that you simply cannot fail at, the freer you will feel to explore things with a sense of adventure.

I FOCUS ON ALL THE THINGS THAT ARE GOOD IN MY LIFE.

How and when to recite this mantra: Recite this mantra three times either out loud or quietly to yourself as often as needed as you close your eyes and visualize all the wonderful things that are happening in your life.

How this mantra can help you: When you focus on all the things that are good in your life, it can instantly make you feel better. But a lot of the time, many of us instead get fixated on all the "bad" things that are happening in life. Thinking of negative things causes your energy to slow down and puts you into a negative state of mind. This mantra reminds you to celebrate the many wonderful things that surround you.

If you are struggling to find good things in your life, start simple. Look to warm sunshine, a gentle breeze, or the roof over your head for something to be grateful for. If you use this mantra for an extended period of time, it will become easier to notice the good things when they arrive. Seemingly bad things are part of life's package deal, but the less focus you give to them and the more you focus on all the positive things in life, the easier and more enjoyable your life will become.

I RELEASE THINGS THAT ARE NO LONGER IN MY CONTROL.

How and when to recite this mantra: Recite this mantra three times either out loud or quietly to yourself as often as needed.

How this mantra can help you: This mantra is perfect to use if you find yourself ruminating about what other people will do or what events will transpire. When you don't stop to check in with yourself, often you find that you are stressing about things that are not really in your control. There is really only one thing you can control in this life and that is you—your responses, thoughts, words, and actions. Everything else is somewhat out of your control. You can't control others, you can't control all the situations you find yourself in, and you can't control the weather! This mantra is designed to remind you of this and help you release all the things that are taking up space in your mind that need to go. There is no point in worrying about things that are not in your control, so give yourself permission to release them. This can do wonders for your stress levels and can help to relieve worrisome and fearful thinking.

Releasing the things you have no control over also helps you to prioritize the things that you *do* have control over. This means that you will have more time to focus on making proactive changes, rather than wasting time obsessing about things you cannot change or have no control over.

I BREATHE INTO FEAR AND TURN IT INTO ADVENTURE.

How and when to recite this mantra: Recite this mantra three times in your mind while breathing in and out deeply. To help shift some of the fear out of your body, you can also shake your hands after reciting the mantra.

How this mantra can help you: We all feel fearful at times and it can truly be debilitating. Fear often arises when you start thinking too far into the future rather than focusing on the present moment. In fact, fear is often entirely a product of your mind rather than reality. When you find yourself in a fearful state, consider instead consciously switching your energy to a more adventurous state. Try to envision whatever you are feeling fearful about as an exciting adventure or as a challenge that you are going to triumph over. Imagine the situation as a video game that you get to work your way through. There are always times in our lives where we have to confront our fears, but often our fears are never as bad as our minds make them out to be. Using this mantra will remind you of this, and will also allow you to look at fearful situations as opportunities for adventure.

I ACCEPT ALL THAT LIFE BRINGS WITH LOVE AND UNDERSTANDING.

How and when to recite this mantra: Recite this mantra three times either out loud or quietly to yourself.

How this mantra can help you: This mantra is perfect to use when you are looking to relieve stress or anxiety and replace it with love, compassion, and understanding. When you view the world through the eyes of love, things instantly change. If, however, you view the world solely through a rational, logical mind then it can be hard to see the good, and it can be hard to make sense of tragedies and hardships. But, when you shift your perspective to a place of the heart, to a place of love and understanding, sometimes things can make more sense and you can trust in the flow of the Universe. When you trust the journey of life, you know that there is a Divine order and timing to everything. This mantra will help you see the world from this place and will remind you to view things from a loving and understanding place as much as possible. Even though this can be hard to do, over time, this mantra will help you to find a new level of compassion for life.

AS I FOCUS ON THE PRESENT, I FEEL AT ONE WITH LIFE.

How and when to recite this mantra: Recite this mantra three times either out loud or quietly to yourself as often as needed.

How this mantra can help you: What does it mean to be present? When you are present, you focus on each moment as it comes. This approach makes things feel more manageable and attainable. When you focus on the past or future, you are dabbling in events beyond your control. When you focus on the present, however, you allow yourself to feel in alignment so that you can take deliberate and conscious action to move forward. In every moment you can decide what you are going to do. This is a very relaxing and comforting place to be in.

This mantra can help you combat feelings of stress and anxiety, and it can even help you to feel more connected to your life rather than feeling swept up in it. By bringing your awareness to the present moment, life can feel a lot simpler and you can feel more connected to the things around you.

I GIVE MYSELF PERMISSION TO LET GO OF WHAT NO LONGER SERVES ME.

How and when to recite this mantra: Recite this mantra five times either out loud or quietly to yourself. For added benefits, you can also write down a list of things that you need to release from your life.

How this mantra can help you: How much old and worn-out baggage are you carrying around? It's a good idea to check in with all areas of your life so that you can make an inventory of what needs to go and what can stay. Simply stating your intention to release things that no longer serve you (as you do when you say this mantra) can set the wheels in motion. Take a few minutes to identify what's holding you back and weighing you down. Life is a continuous process of letting go of old things and welcoming in new things. When you release the old and worn out from your life, you provide space for a brighter beginning. Saying this mantra gives you permission to let go of things, people, and situations that are no longer serving your highest good so you can make room for new and better things.

THINGS ALWAYS HAVE A WAY OF WORKING OUT.

How and when to recite this mantra: Recite this mantra three times either out loud or quietly to yourself as often as needed.

How this mantra can help you: Feeling uncomfortable with a recent development in your life? You're in good company. Still, this uncomfortable feeling can be difficult to live with and can cause heightened feelings of stress, anger, and even frustration. This then causes you to feel overwhelmed and obsessed with finding an immediate solution that is going to magically fix everything. Unfortunately, sometimes that's just not possible. Think back to a challenging time in your life and reflect on how things eventually got sorted. Let that experience reassure you at this difficult time. This mantra is designed to instill trust and faith that everything is going to be okay. As John Lennon famously said, "Everything will be okay in the end. If it's not okay, it's not the end."

It is important to trust and know that no matter how complicated or convoluted a problem seems, there is always a solution and things will always work out as they need to. This mantra will allow you to feel far more relaxed and at ease about your situation so that you can bring more acceptance to your position. It is from this state that problems usually resolve themselves or seem easier to navigate. Have patience. In time, you will see that everything always has a way of working out.

I SURRENDER MY WORRIES TO THE UNIVERSE.

How and when to recite this mantra: Recite this mantra three times either out loud or quietly to yourself as often as needed. Visualize yourself taking your heavy coat of burdens off and handing it over to the Universe to take care of as you recite the words.

How this mantra can help you: Sometimes you just need to release your worries. This is especially true if you find yourself struggling to turn off your mind and relax. Instead, it can be extremely liberating to take a break from any worries and stress and to hand them over to the Universe to take care of. The Universe is always supporting you, and it is there to help you whenever you need it. You just have to have faith and trust that this is in fact the case. In order to build this trust, try surrendering your worries to the Universe and see how it makes you feel. If you notice worrying thoughts creeping back in, remind yourself that the Universe is dealing with them for now and that they are no longer your concern.

Keep reciting this mantra and observe how you begin to feel lighter and more carefree with each passing day. In time, this mantra will help to relieve feelings of stress and will also help you to gain a newfound insight into whatever worries are troubling you.

I DO NOT HAVE TO FIND THE RIGHT ANSWERS; THE RIGHT ANSWERS WILL FIND ME.

How and when to recite this mantra: Recite this mantra three times either out loud or quietly to yourself as often as needed.

How this mantra can help you: This mantra is perfect to use when you are struggling to decide how to address your predicaments or challenges. Sometimes it can seem like your challenges are too big to face, but the truth is you don't have to worry about having them all worked out. Reciting this mantra will help you remember that truth. When you search for the answers to your problems, the task can seem endless and too difficult to manage. It is more rewarding and less stressful, instead, to surrender and allow the right solutions to come to you. If you are an action-oriented person, this may seem like a passive approach—but sometimes a pause is the right decision. This is especially true if you feel like you have been struggling with a problem for a while. By saying this mantra, you are setting an intention to the Universe that you are open to hearing and seeing the right answers so you can move forward. This mantra allows you to become a magnet for the right solutions...so you can stop looking and just start being.

AS I COUNT TO THREE MY WORRIES LEAVE ME...1, 2, 3.

How and when to recite this mantra: Recite this mantra three times either out loud or quietly to yourself whenever you are struggling to release worrisome or stressful thoughts. For added impact, after counting to three, clap your hands or snap your fingers to symbolize the releasing of your worries.

How this mantra can help you: This powerful mantra is designed to help you release your worries and repetitive thoughts so you can feel calm, balanced, and centered. Use it whenever you are feeling overwhelmed or burdened with repetitive thoughts that seem to constantly nag at you. By reciting this mantra, you are giving yourself permission to let go of the thoughts that are keeping you weighed down. Once free of those burdens, you will find clear space in your mind and in your heart. While it can be hard to turn off your thoughts, this mantra helps you to become aware of the thoughts that are serving you and the thoughts that are draining your energy. When you have this awareness, you can then choose to actively focus only on the thoughts that are serving you, lifting you up, and making you feel good. Worrisome thoughts may always be there, but by choosing not to engage in them, you create mental space for focusing on productive solutions and, of course, peace.

CHAPTER 3
MANTRAS FOR SELF-LOVE

These mantras are designed to evoke feelings of love and acceptance for the self so that you can nourish and cherish everything you are. Use these words to bring about positive self-change, and rely on them when you find yourself battling with feelings of low self-esteem.

I ACCEPT WHO I AM. IT IS SAFE FOR ME TO BE MYSELF.

How and when to recite this mantra: Recite this mantra three times either out loud or quietly to yourself. As you recite the words, place your hands over your heart center to help evoke feelings of self-acceptance.

How this mantra can help you: Accepting yourself is about acknowledging your body, your personality, and your traits compassionately and without judgment. Acceptance of yourself is the first step to feeling confident in your body and in your life. Without self-acceptance, it will be very difficult for you to have the confidence you need to go out into the world and do the things that you want to do. Acceptance doesn't mean you can't make changes if you desire; it simply means that you are at peace with who you are and where you are right now. Reciting this mantra will welcome feelings of peace and acceptance into all areas of your life so you can feel uplifted and confident.

This mantra is also perfect to use when you feel fearful of showing the world your true self. Part of your purpose in this life is to live authentically and to be the true you—yet this is impossible to achieve if you have not learned to accept every single part of you, flaws and all. The world is ready to love and accept you, just as you are. The more you believe this and start living as if it were truth, the more you will start to see it mirrored in the world around you.

self-love mantra 2

I AM PERFECT JUST THE WAY I AM.

How and when to recite this mantra: Recite this mantra three times either out loud or quietly to yourself if you are feeling insecure about your body, skills, or talents.

How this mantra can help you: Do you believe that you are perfect just the way you are, or is your mind constantly plagued with all the things that you need to "fix" about yourself? Many of us have grown up with the conditioning that we are just not good enough. We are told that we need to lose weight, gain weight, fix our hair, bulk up, shave this, grow this, wear that...and the list goes on and on. This mantra serves as a reminder that you are doing a great job just as you are and that you don't need to act a certain way or look a certain way in order to be deemed "perfect." These words help you reclaim your power and acknowledge that you are perfect just the way you are.

This mantra also allows you to feel empowered and confident enough to go after what you want without having to wait until you are "good enough" to have it. If you lack self-confidence, it can be easy for you to trick yourself into feeling that you can't have what you want until you have attained some mythical level of perfection. But in truth, it is never too early or too late to go after what you want—you simply need confidence in who you are and the knowledge that you are perfect just the way you are.

I LOVE MYSELF.

How and when to recite this mantra: Recite this mantra one hundred times over the course of a day (or a week if you need more time) until you begin to wholeheartedly believe it.

How this mantra can help you: This is hands down one of the most powerful mantras in this book...but it is also probably the most difficult for people to embrace. Loving yourself is the key to a happy, positive, and fulfilled life, which is why it is so important to say this mantra as often as possible. When you love yourself, everything else in your life has a way of falling into place. This mantra is designed to help you love and appreciate yourself more. Even if you don't a hundred percent believe the words to begin with, the more you say them, the more likely you are to come around to feeling they are true.

Do you find these words uncomfortable to say? If something blocks you from saying this mantra, it can serve as a huge clue as to what is holding you back from achieving happiness in life. Many of us have grown up believing that it is wrong or selfish to love yourself, but this is just not true. Loving yourself is about treating yourself with compassion and kindness. It is thinking so highly of yourself that you would never harm or hurt yourself in any way. When you reach this level of self-love, you will move through life with ease, grace, and authenticity. It also allows you to really tune into your purpose and to feel supported and protected no matter what comes your way.

self-love mantra 4

I CHOOSE TO FEEL GOOD ABOUT MYSELF EVERY DAY.

How and when to recite this mantra: Recite this mantra three times either out loud or quietly to yourself while looking in the mirror.

How this mantra can help you: How you feel about yourself is a choice. You can choose to get hung up on your "flaws," or you can choose to see all the beautiful things about yourself. When you obsess about the things that you hate about your body, it not only puts you in a negative state of mind, but it also amplifies your feelings of self-loathing. When you focus on what you love about your body and allow yourself to feel grateful for all that you have, it boosts your mood, brightens your eyes, and allows you to shine from the inside out.

If you recite this mantra regularly, you will soon become more aware of the thoughts you are carrying about yourself. If you notice negative thoughts about yourself creeping in throughout the day, see if you can replace them with this mantra or switch them to something positive. For example, instead of shaming yourself, consider celebrating all the things you feel grateful for about your body. In the beginning, it may take a while to reprogram those self-loathing thoughts you have been carrying around. You deserve to feel good about yourself, so keep working with this mantra and soon enough those thoughts will be long gone.

I LOVE THE WAY I LOOK AND FEEL. MY BODY IS BEAUTIFUL.

How and when to recite this mantra: Recite this mantra three times either out loud or quietly to yourself while looking at yourself in the mirror. (Naked works best!)

How this mantra can help you: This mantra is another powerful declaration that will boost your feelings of self-confidence and self-esteem. When you love your body and the way you look, your entire mood changes and you feel energized. This mantra is designed to help you feel empowered by the way that you look. You are given only one body, so you may as well love it exactly as it is. This doesn't mean that you can't make changes, but it does mean that you first have to accept and love yourself just as you are. Most of us feel that it is shameful or vain to say that we look beautiful, and many of us even have a hard time accepting compliments about ourselves! Bragging about your looks and honoring your beautiful, amazing, wonderful body are two very different things. The more you say this mantra, the more comfortable you will feel on the inside and on the outside. As you work with this mantra, you may also want to practice being more open and receptive to compliments. When someone compliments what you are wearing or how you look, don't brush it off or play it down; instead, embrace it with a big "Thank you!"

seLf-Love mantra 6

I OPEN MY HEART TO LOVE.

How and when to recite this mantra: Recite this mantra three times either out loud or quietly to yourself as often as needed.

How this mantra can help you: When you feel safe in who you are, you allow yourself to open your heart and welcome in love in all shapes and forms. When you hide yourself away, or close yourself off from the world out of fear or even embarrassment, it becomes very difficult to go out into the world and achieve your dreams and desires. You might also find it difficult to meet people and to put yourself out there in terms of building intimate relationships and establishing friendships. We all have "flaws," but the trick is to not let them define you and to not let them hold you back from doing the things that you want to do. This requires you to accept yourself, flaws and all, and to feel comfortable in the body and with the life you have been given. Feeling comfortable in your skin is so important for a loving and rewarding life, so if you are not there yet, keep working with this mantra. By reciting this mantra as often as possible, you can boost your feelings of comfort with who you are, so you can open your heart to all types of love.

self-love mantra 7

I DESERVE TO FEEL JOYFUL AND POSITIVE.

How and when to recite this mantra: Recite this mantra three times out loud whenever you find yourself feeling guilty about doing things just for pleasure.

How this mantra can help you: You deserve to feel happy and joyful no matter what circumstances come your way. Even though we all go through low times in our lives, feeling joyful and happy is your ultimate purpose in this life. It can be easy to overcomplicate things, but we only get one shot at this life, so why not make it as fun and as exciting as possible? This mantra can help remind you that you deserve joy, and it can instantly put you in a positive and lighter mood, regardless of what is unfolding around you.

This mantra also helps to reprogram any old beliefs you have around having fun and seeking out joyful experiences. Many people feel guilty for doing things that make them feel good, or they feel like life needs to be a struggle, and this mantra helps change that mindset. This mantra is also great to use when you find yourself stuck in a negative rut or have depressive thoughts. The more you recite this mantra, the more you will focus on all the things that are joyful and positive in your life, and the faster you will begin to turn your life around.

I CAN DO WHATEVER I PUT MY MIND TO.

How and when to recite this mantra: Recite this mantra three times either out loud or quietly to yourself when you are trying to get through your to-do list.

How this mantra can help you: Need a boost of motivation? This mantra can provide you with that and so much more. This mantra helps you to believe in yourself and reinforces the idea that nothing is impossible as long as you set your mind to it. The mind is an extremely powerful tool because your beliefs can shape the outcome of your life. If you believe that something good is going to happen, you will look for the good. Just the same, when you think something bad is going to happen, chances are you will find only the bad. This is the power of the mind. The more we can focus on positive thinking, the more our lives will be filled with positivity in return.

I AM SURROUNDED BY LOVE AND LIGHT.

How and when to recite this mantra: Recite this mantra seven to ten times either out loud or quietly to yourself as you visualize a beautiful, protective white light surrounding your entire body.

How this mantra can help you: If you are feeling vulnerable, afraid, or alone, this mantra will help you feel loved and protected. At one time or another we can all find ourselves in situations that feel threatening or uncomfortable. While it is best to remove yourself from these situations as quickly as possible, using this mantra will help you feel protected and safe as you decide on your best course of action.

This mantra can also be used to bring comfort and healing when you are feeling emotionally distressed or fearful about a person or event in your present or future. It is important to know that no matter what, you are never alone and you are always supported by the loving and healing energy of the Universe. Finally, this mantra can be used to boost your mood when you are feeling down about yourself or your life. This mantra is extremely effective at healing and can instantly bring a burst of positive light straight into your heart.

self-love mantra 10

I BELIEVE IN MYSELF.

How and when to recite this mantra: Recite this mantra three times either out loud or quietly to yourself as often as needed.

How this mantra can help you: This mantra is great for helping to motivate you and keep you on track with your goals, dreams, and wishes. You have so much power and potential inside of you, and when you believe in yourself, there really is nothing you can't do and nothing you can't achieve. Believing in yourself also gives you the motivation to keep moving forward and to keep achieving your goals no matter what challenges come your way. In fact, believing in yourself is the foundation to all success. When you don't, you can end up inadvertently doing things to sabotage your efforts, and this in turn can make it harder to reach your goals.

How you talk about your life can also provide clues as to whether or not you are sabotaging yourself. If you say things like "I am going to *try* to do this," you may need to check in with where your intentions really lie. Using the word *try* implies a degree of doubt. Instead, make more affirmative statements, like "I am going to do this." This small alteration can help you shift your vibration to a place of complete self-belief and self-confidence. Using this mantra regularly will remind you to believe in yourself, your abilities, and the determination you have to go after your highest goals, dreams, and wishes.

ONLY LOVE LIVES WITHIN ME.

How and when to recite this mantra: Recite this mantra three times either out loud or quietly to yourself as you place your hands over your heart.

How this mantra can help you: This mantra is designed to remind you of your true essence: love. No matter how many mistakes you have made, love still flows within you. We all have the energy of pure, unconditional love within us and we don't need to do anything other than remember this in order to connect with it. This powerful mantra helps you to tap into the flow of this loving energy, honor it, and even strengthen it.

Using this mantra can also help you clear any emotional barriers you have around your heart or around feelings of love and intimacy in your relationships. It can also help to boost your self-esteem and sense of connectedness with others. This mantra is perfect to use as part of your meditation practice. Meditation helps you to connect with your true inner essence—that stillness and love that lives inside of you—and this mantra can help you to access that essence.

self-love mantra 12

I TRUST MYSELF AND THE DECISIONS THAT I HAVE MADE.

How and when to recite this mantra: Recite this mantra three times either out loud or quietly to yourself.

How this mantra can help you: This mantra is especially useful when you find yourself doubting your actions or decisions you have made. This mantra is about forgiveness, but it is also about helping you learn to trust yourself and trust that you made the right decisions with the knowledge that you had at the time. We all make mistakes and we all do things that we regret, but it is important to understand that, at the time, you did what you did for a reason. Trust in that reason and don't beat yourself up for what you didn't know at the time. Often it is only in hindsight that we can see how our actions have affected us. Beating yourself up for things you did in the past puts you in a negative head-space and makes it difficult for you to focus on anything positive.

This mantra is a good one to turn to when you find yourself holding on to the past. You can't change the past, but you can change your future through letting go and forgiving.

self-love mantra 13

I AM DOING THE BEST I CAN WITH WHAT I KNOW.

How and when to recite this mantra: Recite this mantra three times either out loud or quietly to yourself.

How this mantra can help you: How do you view others' behavior versus your own? Often we are very quick to give the benefit of the doubt to other people, but when it comes to ourselves, we can be harsh and unforgiving. Use this mantra whenever you are feeling doubtful of your abilities or when you are learning something new. This mantra is there to remind you that you are still in the learning phase and that you don't need to master the skill immediately.

It is helpful to remember that, in life, we are all just getting by to the best of our abilities based on the information and the beliefs we have. The energy of the words in this mantra will encourage you to keep moving forward and to stay confident in yourself and the learning process. At the end of the day, the more faith and confidence you have in your abilities, the easier it will be for you to get the hang of things.

This mantra is also effective when you need to forgive yourself or others for something. It can be hard to forgive mistakes, but if you remember that everyone, including you, is just doing the best that they can with what they know, then you will be able to see the situation from a compassionate place. This can make finding forgiveness a lot easier. Forgiveness is extremely healing and can help to set you free.

self-love mantra 14

I HAVE THE POWER TO MAKE THE CHANGES I DESIRE.

How and when to recite this mantra: Recite this mantra nine times either out loud or quietly to yourself.

How this mantra can help you: Ready to make powerful changes in your life? If so, this mantra is for you. Sometimes we want to make changes in our lives but we are not sure if we can really do it. This mantra serves as a reminder that you do, in fact, have the power to make the changes that you want. You may not feel like it just yet, but, over time, chanting these words will help to inspire you to take the right actions moving forward. Reciting this mantra can also help you to feel sure of yourself. Changes, both big and small, can feel scary and nerve-wracking, but all you need to do is trust that you have the strength and courage to get through it all.

To help with the process, it may be beneficial to write a list of the things that you would like to change or welcome into your life. This may help you to develop a clearer understanding of which changes you feel empowered to make and which ones may still need more time to develop.

self-love mantra 15

LOVING MYSELF ALLOWS ME TO GIVE MORE TO OTHERS.

How and when to recite this mantra: Recite this mantra three times either out loud or quietly to yourself as you place your hands into a prayer position over your heart.

How this mantra can help you: Do you have a hard time putting your own needs first? Do you have a hard time saying no to others? Many people feel guilty for putting their own needs first or get stuck in a programmed pattern of putting other people before themselves. While this is sometimes necessary, operating your life in this way all the time is eventually going to lead to burnout and feelings of resentment. This mantra is designed to help remind you that the more you love yourself and the more you are able to put yourself first, the more you will be able to give to others. When you love yourself and take care of your needs first, you give yourself more energy to give out to others. As the old saying goes, "You can't pour from an empty cup." Instead, fill your own cup first and then you can pour into others'.

To fill your own cup, you have to learn to love yourself and listen to what your heart, body, and mind need from you. Take a moment to still your mind, and then ask yourself what you really need right now. Do you need to take a nap? Do you need to exercise? Whatever the answer may be, be sure to follow through on it. Also be sure to check in with yourself like this on a regular basis.

I HAVE THE COURAGE TO GET THROUGH WHATEVER LIFE BRINGS.

How and when to recite this mantra: Recite this mantra three times either out loud or quietly to yourself. For added benefits, recite this mantra while looking straight into your eyes in a mirror. This will help to evoke feelings of courage.

How this mantra can help you: Life often generates challenging situations that can make you feel fearful or full of dread. This mantra is designed to give you a boost of courage so that you can conquer whatever comes your way. You have the innate courage to get through any situation that comes your way; all you need to do is believe it and put one foot in front of the other. By stating this mantra and really believing the words, you can ease your fears and worries and reprogram your mind to focus on self-assurance rather than self-doubt. Doubt is one of the biggest contributors to fear, and when you can release any doubtful or negative thoughts, you will naturally feel more confident. Sometimes the only way you can release an emotion like fear is by allowing yourself to feel it but then moving forward anyway. This mantra will help inspire you to take action and will allow you the boost of courage you need to "feel the fear but do it anyway."

self-love mantra 17

I AM EXACTLY WHERE I NEED TO BE.

How and when to recite this mantra: Recite this mantra three times either out loud or quietly to yourself.

How this mantra can help you: Do you feel content and happy with where you are in life? Many of us move through our lives wishing we were in a different place or wishing we were experiencing a different set of circumstances. We feel unsatisfied with our lives but get stuck in our day-to-day existences and find it hard to make a switch. Even though there is always room to make changes, sometimes you also just have to accept where you are in life and know that it is where you are meant to be (at least for now). There is a great power in simply believing that you are right where you need to be on your path.

This mantra is valuable when you feel stuck at a dead end in your life. Feeling stuck is a sign that you are meant to learn or discover something where you currently are. This requires you to have some patience, however. This mantra can help you clear your mind and get you focused on the positive while you wait for the right guidance to come.

SeLF-LOVe mantra 18

EVERYTHING IS ALWAYS WORKING OUT FOR MY HIGHEST GOOD.

How and when to recite this mantra: Recite this mantra three times either out loud or quietly to yourself.

How this mantra can help you: It is important to believe that everything is always working out for your highest good. Why? This line of thinking instantly shifts you into a positive place and allows you to feel supported by life rather than feel like a victim. Even if things are not going the way you would like them to, taking this positive approach can help you focus on the bright side and see solutions rather than problems. Looking at life from this point of view also makes life far less stressful and so much more manageable. As the spiritual author Wayne Dyer said, "With everything that has happened to you, you can either feel sorry for yourself or treat what has happened as a gift. Everything is either an opportunity to grow or an obstacle to keep you from growing. You get to choose." Choosing to see things as gifts makes life so much easier to bear and so much more enjoyable. Reciting this mantra will shift your mind to a more positive way of thinking and will bring your awareness to all the things that are working in your favor rather than against you.

I RELEASE MY PAST AND FORGIVE MYSELF.

How and when to recite this mantra: Recite this mantra five times either out loud or quietly to yourself as you place your hands over your heart.

How this mantra can help you: This mantra relieves feelings of guilt and shame from events that occurred in the past. Forgiving yourself is one of the most loving and healing things you can do, and it can instantly make you feel lighter, more confident, and more positive. Forgiveness can also help you to release blocked or stuck energy that you are holding on to from your past. Practicing forgiveness will free you from the past and open up your energy so that you can receive new opportunities as well. The words in this mantra are meant to replace any guilty or shameful feelings with love and compassion for yourself. This mantra can help you view yourself and those around you with more compassion and unconditional love. You deserve your own forgiveness, and this mantra will help you achieve just that.

CHAPTER 4

MANTRAS FOR HEALING

These mantras are designed to stimulate healing for your mind, body, and spirit so you can feel balanced, healthy, and in control of your well-being. Use these mantras during times of illness or when you're suffering through emotional or spiritual traumas.

Healing Mantra 1

I FEEL HEALTHY AND RADIANT IN MY BODY, MIND, AND SOUL.

How and when to recite this mantra: Recite this mantra seven times either out loud or quietly to yourself while placing your hands over your heart.

How this mantra can help you: When you feel radiant, your entire being shines with a glow and inner light. Your energy becomes infectious, and you feel abundant and joyful as you move through life. This mantra is designed to help boost your feelings of radiance and evoke the energy of healing. Did you know that the most powerful way to heal yourself is to change the way you choose to look at things? We may not always be able to choose what happens to us, but we can choose how we feel about it. The more positive and uplifted you feel, the more likely it will be that your body, mind, and soul will be able to heal. This mantra is designed to help you focus on all the things that are going right with your body, mind, and soul so you don't become fixated on all the things that might be going wrong. This mantra instantly creates feelings of wellness and allows you to feel whole, balanced, and restored.

Repeating this mantra regularly also helps you to feel empowered by your state of being rather than pushed into despair. Often when we are battling an illness, whether it is physical or mental, it can be difficult to feel empowered. But the words in this mantra can empower you and make a huge difference.

HEALING MANTRA 2

I GIVE THANKS TO EVERY CELL IN MY AMAZING BODY.

How and when to recite this mantra: Recite this mantra three times either out loud or quietly to yourself. As you recite this mantra, visualize your body being in a radiant, healthy, and strong state from head to toe.

How this mantra can help you: How often do you stop and thank your body for its hard work? How often do you pay attention to the amazing miracle that is your physical body? Every minute of every day, your body is performing millions of tasks on a cellular level in order to help keep you alive, active, and well. Every second of every day, your body is using its innate intelligence to heal your ailments and alert you when something is not quite right. Your body is intelligent, dedicated, and hardworking—sometimes a little thanks is in order! This mantra is designed to bring healing grace to your body and to thank it for all that it does. Giving thanks for your body helps to raise your energetic vibration, and this in itself can be extremely healing and therapeutic.

As you work with this mantra, you may also want to highlight particular areas of your body that you are most thankful for. This can be especially beneficial if you have an illness that is affecting one part or one side of your body. Thanking your body can help you to feel empowered and comforted at a time when it's difficult to feel in control of what's happening. It can also help guide your body even further along on the healing process.

I CELEBRATE MY BODY AND KNOW THAT IT IS HEALED.

How and when to recite this mantra: Recite this mantra three times either out loud or quietly to yourself while placing your hand over your heart.

How this mantra can help you: Your body is an amazing Divine instrument, and the more you can honor it and thank it, the more positive your mindset becomes. Having a positive attitude can drastically improve the healing process. The more you say this mantra, the more you will begin to feel confident, healed, and at peace with your situation, no matter what is going on.

For added benefits, you may also want to "celebrate" your body by taking time out to do something relaxing and pampering. Perhaps treat yourself to a massage or to a pedicure, maybe even adorn your body with a new set of clothes. Celebrate your body in big and small ways and notice how uplifted and inspired it makes you feel.

HEALING MANTRA 4

THE MORE I LOVE AND SUPPORT MYSELF, THE MORE I HEAL.

How and when to recite this mantra: Recite this mantra four times either out loud or quietly to yourself while you place your hands in a prayer position over your heart. Use it whenever you are feeling down about your health on a physical, emotional, or mental level.

How this mantra can help you: This mantra is a powerful reminder that the more you love and honor yourself, and the more intently you listen to your body, the easier it is to heal. Self-love is vitally important on the healing journey. If you don't listen to your body and trust your instincts, you could miss important signs your body is sending you. When you love yourself, you also encourage the kind of compassion and care that you would extend to any other loved one. This energy then filters through your body and can feel extremely comforting and relaxing.

Stress can create or exacerbate many types of medical issues, but self-love and being gentle with yourself are great ways to avoid stress. You can also use this mantra as a support when you are responsible for caring for the well-being of others, which can be very stressful. As a caregiver for others, it is important that you look after your own body and check in with yourself to make sure that your own needs are being met. After all, if you are not looking after yourself it will be very difficult for you to look after someone else.

WITH EVERY EXHALE, I RELEASE ALL DIS-EASE FROM MY BODY.

How and when to recite this mantra: Recite this mantra five times either out loud or quietly to yourself while focusing on your breath. As you say the mantra, inhale and then exhale deeply. Visualize any discomfort or dis-ease leaving your body like a cloud of smoke.

How this mantra can help you: Disease is simply dis-ease (meaning a lack of ease), and it can arrive in many forms. Sometimes it is physical; other times it is emotional. Whenever dis-ease enters your body, your breath can be a wonderful tool to help you restore balance and harmony. In fact, working with your breath can help to replace dis-ease with ease. Reciting this mantra reminds you to use your breath to help bring a sense of peace and stillness to your body.

This mantra is also extremely empowering because you will feel that you are taking your health into your own hands. This is an important part of any healing journey, because no one can take true responsibility for your health except you. Doctors and other medical professionals can only do so much—beyond that, you need to take the steps and actions to support your own healing process. You may also want to keep a journal in order to track your progress and release any pent-up thoughts or emotions that come to the surface after you have done your breath work. When you do releasing work like this, sometimes it can bring past pains to the surface, and writing can be a therapeutic way to release them.

Healing mantra 6

MY BODY IS HEALTHY, MY MIND IS STRONG, AND MY HEART IS FULL.

How and when to recite this mantra: Recite this mantra three times either out loud or quietly to yourself while standing straight and tall with your hands in a prayer position over your heart. This will evoke feelings of strength, power, and gratitude.

How this mantra can help you: This is the perfect mantra to use to evoke feelings of health, wellness, and prosperity. Your body, mind, and heart are powerful tools for healing, and building up each of them can do amazing things for your overall healing journey. In fact, many cultures believe that true health is achieved when your body, mind, and heart are in balance with each other. Along with helping to achieve balance in these three areas, this mantra is designed to empower you and shift your mindset to a place of positivity and hope. Over time, reciting this mantra will also help you feel better from within, which will then give you the confidence you need to live the life that you truly desire. When you feel stronger in your body, mind, and heart you can be more connected with who you really are.

MY BODY CONTAINS DIVINE WISDOM TO HEAL ITSELF.

How and when to recite this mantra: Recite this mantra eleven times either out loud or quietly to yourself. To really feel the words, you can also practice saying this mantra with your eyes closed and your hands over your heart or in a prayer position. If you are currently taking any medications, you can also recite this mantra as you take them as a way of supporting their effect on the body.

How this mantra can help you: Your body is an incredible source of knowledge and wisdom. When you cut yourself, your body knows exactly what to do to heal the wound; when you catch a cold, your body has all the tools it needs to fight it off. Yet it's easy to forget that all of this Divine wisdom is living inside of you all the time because you don't have to think about it for healing to happen. Taking a moment to reflect on this can be truly empowering and can remind you that your body is extremely intelligent, powerful, and even magical. Reciting this mantra will help you put faith and trust back into the healing abilities of your body. This in turn can help you to feel more empowered on your healing journey and can put you in a more positive frame of mind whenever disease or illness comes your way. This mantra also allows you to trust yourself and your body's own ability to heal. Use this mantra as part of your healing process to help support and enhance all of your other efforts and medical interventions.

HEALING MANTRA 8

EVERY DAY I GROW STRONGER IN NEW WAYS.

How and when to recite this mantra: Recite this mantra three times either out loud or quietly to yourself.

How this mantra can help you: Do you need more stamina to help you get through the day? This mantra is designed to help you regain your strength and find your inner power. We all have the ability to stand strong and be powerful in our own ways, and this mantra is there to guide you. When you are feeling down or low, this mantra can also serve as a reminder that even though things seem bleak, you are in the process of getting stronger. This mantra may even help to remind you of a time when you overcame an obstacle or when you were able to face your fears. That memory may just be enough to inspire you to get through a low point of your life. Sometimes growing into our fullest potential takes time, but with every passing day you can get stronger with the help of this mantra. Remind yourself that you are getting there, even if progress happens little by little. You are a strong, vibrant, healthy being, and this mantra will lead you to rediscover this.

I AM WHOLE; I AM BALANCED; I AM IN PERFECT ALIGNMENT.

How and when to recite this mantra: Recite this mantra three times either out loud or quietly to yourself whenever you need to feel calm, balanced, and in harmony with your life. Take three to five deep breaths in and out after you recite the words.

How this mantra can help you: This powerful mantra can instantly help bring you back to your center and back to a place of stillness. Life can sometimes push you to have feelings all over the place, but this mantra reminds you that regardless of what is happening on the outside, inside you are still a whole and perfect being who has everything you need. This mantra is there to guide you through the chaos and remind you that true peace and happiness must come from within. Of course, it can be easy to feel at peace when everything is going well. But when things are turned upside down, you will face the true test of whether or not you can find your sense of peace and restore balance and harmony to your life. If you need a helping hand, reach for this mantra. It is there to help you, and it can immediately provide you with feelings of alignment.

I ACCEPT MYSELF EXACTLY AS I AM.

How and when to recite this mantra: Recite this mantra eleven times either out loud or quietly to yourself. For added benefits, say this mantra while looking at yourself in the mirror.

How this mantra can help you: We all have things that we would like to improve in our lives, whether it is our appearance, our income, our education level, or our job. Even though it is perfectly acceptable to have higher ambitions for yourself, it is important to not confuse these ambitions with a lack of self-acceptance. True self-acceptance is something that is measured on the inside and is dictated by how you feel about yourself, regardless of your circumstances and appearance. When you truly accept yourself, your whole world shines and becomes a far more comfortable and loving place to be in. When you struggle to accept yourself, however, nothing can feel good enough and life will always feel uncomfortable. This mantra is designed to help you accept yourself on the deepest of levels so that you can live from a place of complete authenticity. When you accept yourself, you give yourself permission to be who you are and to shine your light into the world. This is a powerful state to live from and it allows you the freedom to go after all of your goals and ambitions with purpose.

I WELCOME HEALTH AND HAPPINESS INTO MY LIFE.

How and when to recite this mantra: Recite this mantra nine times either out loud or quietly to yourself.

How this mantra can help you: Think of this mantra as an invitation to health and happiness. Sometimes you have to invite these qualities into your life to remind yourself that they exist and that you are deserving of them. By reciting this mantra, you will open the doorway to welcome health and happiness into your life so that you can feel joyful, abundant, and full of life. Even though you don't really *need* to invite these things into your life (they're already there!), you might need to rediscover them. This mantra encourages you to do that. As you welcome health and happiness back into your life, make a list of all the things that actually make you feel happy and healthy. Making this list helps you to reflect on what fills you up. This process also directs your awareness toward what you need to bring more of into your life. When you embrace all the things that enrich your life and bring you feelings of health and joy, you will feel more connected to these states of being. This, in turn, will align your energetic vibration so that you may receive even more health and happiness.

AS I HEAL, MAY I BE A SOURCE OF HEALING FOR OTHERS.

How and when to recite this mantra: Recite this mantra three times either out loud or quietly to yourself with your hands in prayer position.

How this mantra can help you: This mantra is perfect to use when you are responsible for caring for others or when you wish to help, guide, or heal others. You have your own healing powers, and this mantra is designed to help you unlock and discover what they are. One of the easiest ways to understand your personal healing powers is by thinking about what you have healed in your life already. You can pass along this wisdom to others who are on their own healing journeys. This mantra is there to remind you that as you heal you are also developing the healing tools to help those around you. When you heal, those around you also benefit organically, especially those who are close to you and those who look up to you.

I LISTEN TO MY BODY AND RESPOND TO ITS NEEDS.

How and when to recite this mantra: Recite this mantra three times either out loud or quietly to yourself with your eyes closed. For added benefits, you can also place your hands over your heart as you recite the words.

How this mantra can help you: This mantra is perfect to use when you want to tune into your body, mind, and soul. Your body is always speaking to you; the trick is to silence your mind so that you can tune into the wisdom and intuitive messages that are coming to you from within. Reciting this mantra serves as a reminder to always listen to your body and pay attention to any signs or clues it may offer. Sometimes these clues and signs can be subtle (such as feeling thirsty or hungry), and other times these signs and clues can be much louder (such as muscle pain or a sore throat). By listening to your body and observing without judgment, you put yourself in the best possible position to know what your body truly needs and desires in any given moment. Over time, this mantra can help you to become more sensitive to the needs of your body so that you can be sure you are never doing any harm to it.

This mantra can also help you if you are looking to adopt a healthier lifestyle or eating plan. By tuning into your body, you will have a better understanding of the nutrients and food your body needs and when your body needs to stretch or exercise.

I HAVE THE POWER TO MAKE CHANGES THAT WILL IMPROVE MY HEALTH.

How and when to recite this mantra: Recite this mantra three times either out loud or quietly to yourself.

How this mantra can help you: This mantra is perfect to use when you are looking to make productive changes to your health, such as giving up an addictive habit or going on a new diet or eating plan. This mantra also allows you to shift your mindset to a place of inspiration and motivation instead of self-judgment. This mantra will also give you the persistence and willpower you need to stick with a healthy lifestyle plan, especially for the truly challenging ones like quitting smoking or staying on a new diet. You may not be able to control what happens to you, but you can control how you react to things, and taking ownership of your health is one of the most powerful and rewarding things you can do.

I KNOW THAT I AM BEING GUIDED ON MY HEALING JOURNEY.

How and when to recite this mantra: Recite this mantra three times either out loud or quietly to yourself while placing your hands over your heart.

How this mantra can help you: The Universe is always on your side and is always sending you signs and clues that are guiding you in the right direction. When you are going through a period of healing, whether on a physical or emotional level, it is common to feel alone or isolated. Perhaps you feel that no one really understands or gets what you are going through. This mantra is designed to remind you that you are always being guided, no matter how alone or lonely you may feel on your journey. Open up your awareness to all of the signs and clues the Universe may be sending your way. These signs and clues are often felt on an intuitive level, but this mantra will help open you up so you can listen too. Reaching out to the Universe for help on your healing path can be extremely powerful, and this mantra can be part of the process. We are all guided in this life, whether we realize it or appreciate it, and this mantra helps you honor that. Over time, these words can also help you restore feelings of hope, faith, and optimism on your healing journey.

EVERYTHING I NEED TO HEAL IS ALREADY WITHIN ME.

How and when to recite this mantra: Recite this mantra five times either out loud or quietly to yourself while placing your hands over your heart.

How this mantra can help you: Everything you need is inside of you, and this includes all the things you need to heal. This mantra is powerful because it reminds you of the wisdom and strength of your body, mind, and soul. You are already whole and you are already complete—all you need to do is remember this.

This mantra can also help you shift your mindset so you can claim some of your personal healing power back. While at times we need medical intervention in order to heal, all too often we give our power away to these medications and lose trust within ourselves. This doesn't mean that we need to stop seeking outside help, but rather it means we need to seek outside help with the knowledge that we also have help from within. This mantra is there to remind you that no matter what, you have the power within to know the right way forward. All you need to do is silence your mind and tune into your intuition. This can be tricky to do at first, but with regular mindfulness practices like meditation and reciting mantras, it will become easier.

Healing mantra 17

I RELEASE ANY DRAMA AND REPLACE IT WITH PEACE.

How and when to recite this mantra: Recite this mantra three times either out loud or quietly to yourself.

How this mantra can help you: This mantra is perfect to use when you feel yourself getting swept away in petty dramas, gossip, and bickering. It is very easy to become caught up in the drama around you. Often we even find ourselves tangled up in drama that is not even ours! Instead of getting sucked into the drama around you, it is much more powerful to find your peace and simplify your life. This mantra will bring you to a place of peace and serenity. It can be hard at times to disengage from the drama around you, but these words can help you do that. They will even allow you to see things from a higher perspective. When you view things from a higher perspective, solutions become more apparent and feelings of stress and anxiety are reduced. This is a simple mantra, but definitely a very powerful one.

HeaLInG manTRa 18

I WILL BE KIND TO MYSELF.
I WILL TAKE CARE OF
MY NEEDS BEFORE OTHERS'.

How and when to recite this mantra: Recite this mantra three times either out loud or quietly to yourself.

How this mantra can help you: While giving is good, if you are giving to the detriment of your own health and well-being, then what you are offering is never going to be of value to anyone. This mantra is perfect to use when you are feeling compromised or when you have been giving too much of your time and energy away to other people. If you are feeling guilty about saying no to others, these words can help you to reclaim your own self-worth and self-esteem and break your habit of always saying yes to others in order to be accepted. Often when you look beneath the surface, giving away your time and energy to others is a sign of insecurity or that you feel like you need to give to others in order to be liked or accepted. By stating this mantra, you will learn to be kinder to yourself and to value yourself more, which is something that we all need to be better at doing.

I OXYGENATE MY BODY THROUGH FRESH AIR, LAUGHTER, AND EXERCISE.

How and when to recite this mantra: Recite this mantra three times either out loud or quietly to yourself. As you say the words, focus on your breath. As you inhale you can visualize your body becoming lighter, more energized, and more confident.

How this mantra can help you: This mantra is perfect for giving you a boost of energy and revitalizing your mind, body, and spirit. This mantra is designed to give you an instant pick-me-up and will help you tackle the day ahead with gusto. Oxygenating your body through taking deep breaths, exercising, and drinking plenty of water is extremely beneficial and can help awaken your entire body. Reciting this mantra will remind you of your ability to create energy. It will also help you wake up your body so that you can achieve all that you hope to during the day.

Another benefit of this mantra is that it reminds you to emphasize things like laughter and getting regular exercise. These are both very important factors in the health and well-being of your body and can make a world of difference when you're going through a period of healing. Laughter has long been regarded as the best form of medicine, and we all know about the copious benefits that exercise can also have. Both of these activities are extremely oxygenating and have healing benefits beyond the physical. By bringing awareness to these small but significant activities, you can make meaningful progress on all levels of healing.

CHAPTER 5
MANTRAS FOR SUCCESS

These mantras will boost feelings of success and confidence in all areas of your life so that you will have the willpower and motivation to fulfill your wildest dreams. Use these mantras when you need to push forward in your career or achieve your personal goals, or when you simply need some words of loving encouragement.

I AM STRONG AND CONFIDENT IN EVERYTHING I DO.

How and when to recite this mantra: Recite this mantra three times out loud while standing or sitting up straight. As you say the words, be sure to feel the strength of your body.

How this mantra can help you: Do you need a boost of confidence? When you feel confident, you carry yourself with an entirely different energy. Your motivation levels increase, you become more determined and driven, and your productivity also increases. When you feel confident, you also feel like you have more freedom to take calculated risks, speak your truth, and take a leap of faith. In fact, confidence is one of the main ingredients in the recipe for building a successful life.

Along with reciting this mantra, it may help to pay extra attention to the activities that make you feel confident. Be sure that you spend time doing them. We all have things that we are good at, and focusing on them can naturally build up feelings of confidence. This mantra is also perfect to use when starting a new job, when learning something new, or when you are taking an exam or a test.

I KNOW I CAN ACHIEVE ALL OF MY DREAMS.

How and when to recite this mantra: Recite this mantra three times either out loud or quietly to yourself.

How this mantra can help you: Having a dream gives you ambition and purpose, but sometimes dreams feel difficult or even impossible to achieve. This mantra is designed to help you turn your dreams into realities. By regularly stating that you know you can achieve your dreams, you shift your mindset to a positive place that allows you to focus on all the things you can do rather than the things you can't. When you work from this place, it becomes a lot easier to overcome obstacles and drop any fears you may have around achieving your goals. Over time, working from this state of being can help you to find the motivation and inspiration you need to bring your dreams to life.

This mantra is particularly useful whenever you have doubts about any aspect of your dreams or goals. When you notice a doubtful thought arising, practice saying this mantra instead. See how it helps reprogram your mind to a place of success. Doubts are common, but the more you become aware of them and the more you replace them with something positive and hopeful, the more successful you will feel.

I RELEASE ANY LIMITS I PLACE ON MYSELF AND KNOW THAT ALL THINGS ARE POSSIBLE.

How and when to recite this mantra: Recite this mantra three times either out loud or quietly to yourself. For added benefits, place your hands over your heart as you repeat this mantra.

How this mantra can help you: How many times have you had a great, inspired idea only to have it shut down by a fearful thought? We all have self-limiting beliefs and fears, but sometimes it is necessary to push them aside in order to go after what we really want. This mantra is there to remind you that self-limiting beliefs are simply just self-programmed ideas that have developed over time. The good news is that they can be reprogrammed. When you release your limitations and replace them with possibilities, there is truly nothing you can't accomplish. Use this mantra whenever doubtful thoughts or fears start creeping in and begin blocking you from achieving your goals.

success mantra 4

WHEN I AM TRUE TO MYSELF, I ALIGN WITH MY PURPOSE.

How and when to recite this mantra: Recite this mantra five times either out loud or quietly to yourself while placing your hands in a prayer position over your heart.

How this mantra can help you: Your purpose in this life is simply to be yourself. The only way you can do this is if you know yourself. Knowing yourself is about living from a place of authenticity and always honoring your truth. This means learning how to tune into your true intentions, standing up for yourself, and responding to yourself and others with love and compassion. When you are true to yourself, then the right job, the right partner, and the right life decisions automatically follow. When you are true to yourself, you are automatically connected to your purpose and feelings of fulfillment.

Your truth arises from deep within your heart, and the words in this mantra will help you follow your heart and your truth with ease. This mantra can also be used to remind you that your purpose is not something you need to go in search of, but rather it is connected to your inner truth—it's already inside you. As author of *Dying to Be Me,* Anita Moorjani said, "Your only purpose is to be yourself, otherwise you deprive the universe of who you came here to be." Whenever you are feeling out of balance or like you are not living up to your purpose, recite this mantra and see what a difference it can make.

I FEEL SUCCESSFUL IN ALL AREAS OF MY LIFE.

How and when to recite this mantra: Recite this mantra three times either out loud or quietly to yourself.

How this mantra can help you: Everyone has his or her own definition of success, but if you are living and breathing, then you are already successful in the eyes of the Universe. Take a moment to think about your definition of success. No matter what your answer is, in order to bring more of it into your life you first need to *feel* all the emotions you associate with success. Reciting this mantra brings your awareness to the feelings of success that are already present in your life, both big and small. The mind is an extremely powerful thing, and the more you can feel and honor your current successes and recognize your successes even in your failures, the more you will start opening up your energy to welcoming in all that you desire. This mantra is perfect to use when you are looking to increase your feelings of success or when you are encountering a failure of some kind. By reciting this mantra, you will always feel hopeful and bountiful in all areas of your life.

I DESERVE A LIFE THAT FEELS AWESOME ON EVERY LEVEL.

How and when to recite this mantra: Recite this mantra three times either out loud or quietly to yourself.

How this mantra can help you: You deserve an incredible, amazing, and abundant life, and this mantra is here to remind you of this! Reciting this mantra will help you feel positive and excited about your life again, and it will remind you that life is meant to be a fun adventure. Even through moments of adversity in life, these words will have you looking on the bright side. They will also help you focus on all the things you can do to feel good again. There is a lot of power in knowing that you deserve an awesome life, and by reciting this mantra, you will slowly begin to realize this. You may even receive the inspiration to let go of things that don't make your life awesome so that you can make room for the things that do.

Everyone on this planet deserves to live an awesome life, and you are no exception. The more you know and believe this, the more awesomeness will flow into your life. In time, this mantra can also help you to take actions and make changes in order to create a life that feels awesome on both the inside and outside.

I FIND WAYS TO FEEL PASSIONATE EVERY SINGLE DAY.

How and when to recite this mantra: Recite this mantra three times either out loud or quietly to yourself. For added benefits, after reciting this mantra, make a list of one to five things you feel passionate about that you can bring into your life today.

How this mantra can help you: It is so important to find time for the things that you feel passionate about. Your passions hold clues as to what makes you come alive. These passions also show you where you can find more joy in your life. If you don't know what you feel passionate about, then it is also important for you to make the time to figure it out. A passion is anything that makes you feel alive, so find whatever inspires you (no matter how small or how grand) and make a point to bring more of it into your life. Making time to do the things that you feel passionate about on a daily basis can help energize your life and can make you feel more inspired and more positive. Reciting this mantra will remind you to bring more passion into your life and to find the fun again, which is so important for any healthy lifestyle. In fact, making time for fun and your passions is crucial when it comes to living a positive life that feels successful and rewarding.

success mantra 8

THINGS ARE ALWAYS WORKING OUT IN MY FAVOR.

How and when to recite this mantra: Recite this mantra three times either out loud or quietly to yourself.

How this mantra can help you: Things always have a way of working out, even if they don't always go how you expect them to. If you are feeling uncertain or stressed about a decision or upcoming event, chant these words. You will be reminded that no matter what, everything is going to be okay and there are solutions for whatever problems come your way. Reciting these powerful words also helps to reprogram your mind so that you can see the world as a loving, generous place rather than as a place full of corruption and hostility. Choosing to see the world in a positive light can increase your feelings of motivation and joy, which can allow you to live life to the fullest. Even if things don't appear to be working out in your favor at first, reciting this mantra can help you to see things from different points of view. This then allows you to see the benefits in all situations that come your way. Life rarely goes according to plan, but it does help to know that things are always working out in your favor, as long as you believe that they are.

success mantra 9

I GIVE MYSELF PERMISSION TO SUCCEED.

How and when to recite this mantra: Recite this mantra three times either out loud or quietly to yourself. After reciting the mantra, close your eyes and visualize yourself succeeding at any goals you may be currently working toward.

How this mantra can help you: It is very common to be afraid of success. In fact, ironically, most people fear success more than they fear failure. This is because failure is often far more comfortable or familiar than actually reaching a place of success. This may seem counterintuitive, but it is interesting to note that many people expect to fail, which is why success can feel so scary. Success can be the "unknown," and achieving this state can bring up a whole host of other insecurities and fears. If you find yourself fearing success or feeling like you are not worthy of success, this is a good mantra to try. Reciting these words on a regular basis will help you develop a more positive attitude and take a more "can-do" approach to life. This mentality will give you the courage you need to go after your dreams and to pursue whatever you desire without fear. When you stop fearing success, you can achieve it, and this mantra is there to remind you that you are worthy of all the success in the world.

I TAKE A LEAP OF FAITH IN THE DIRECTION OF MY DREAMS.

How and when to recite this mantra: Recite this mantra five times either out loud or quietly to yourself. After reciting the mantra, take a moment to close your eyes and visualize your dreams coming to fruition.

How this mantra can help you: Sometimes in order to find success, you have to be brave. You may have heard the saying, "Success favors the bold." There is a lot of truth to this statement. If you want to reach new heights in your life, you need to be willing to take calculated risks. This mantra is perfect to use when you have reached this point in your life and you just need that extra push in conquering your fears to go after your dreams and take that leap of faith into new territory. Whether you are looking to start a new business, travel to an exotic destination, or quit your job and pursue something else, this mantra is there to help.

The words in this mantra will reduce your feelings of fear around taking action and, instead, will help reprogram your mind to focus on trusting yourself and having faith. After all, the more faith you have in yourself, the higher you will be able to climb and the more likely you will be to actually take that leap of faith.

success mantra 11

NEW DOORS ARE ALWAYS OPENING FOR ME.

How and when to recite this mantra: Recite this mantra three times either out loud or quietly to yourself.

How this mantra can help you: Do you ever feel like you are encountering road block after road block in life? When this happens it can leave you feeling confused, frustrated, and even uncertain about the future. If you find yourself hitting many dead ends, turn to these words. Reciting this mantra will help to ease your worries and will reprogram your mind to focus on new opportunities. Sometimes it is easy to get stuck and become trapped in a limited mindset. From this place, it can be challenging to see new opportunities when they arrive. Sometimes our high or low expectations can also cause us to miss what is right in front of our noses. This mantra can help you shift things so that you can see new potential that perhaps you never noticed before. If you are at an ending to a particular point in your life, this mantra will also help you have the faith that a new door will be opening for you very soon.

I SEE FAILURE AS AN OPPORTUNITY.

How and when to recite this mantra: Recite this mantra three times either out loud or quietly to yourself.

How this mantra can help you: Have you ever considered that what you perceive to be a failure may actually be a success? Just because things don't go the way you thought they would, or just because you have made a few mistakes, doesn't mean that you have failed. There are successes to be found in every failure, and there are new lessons to be learned in every situation. Failures are understandably very disappointing, but if you change the way you look at your failure, you may see an opportunity or a potential that wasn't there before. Failures allow you to learn and grow. Failures actually shape you into who you are and allow you to become stronger, wiser, and more confident in your abilities. The words in this mantra will help to shift your mindset so that you can see the positive side of failure and focus on all the opportunities that have arisen because of it. This is a very powerful mantra that will help you look on the bright side.

IT IS NEVER TOO LATE TO MAKE A CHANGE.

How and when to recite this mantra: Recite this mantra seven times either out loud or quietly to yourself.

How this mantra can help you: When you have been living your life a certain way for a long period of time, it can feel very challenging to make changes. However, it is never too late to change or to overhaul your life—all you need is faith, trust, and motivation to make it happen. No matter what, you have the power, strength, and courage to make the changes that you desire. Change can be scary, but step by step and day by day you can make the progress that you have been longing to make. The more you recite this mantra, the more your confidence will build and the more energy and strength you will have to put your plans into action so you can lead the life that you long to lead.

success mantra 14

I CREATE SPACE IN MY LIFE FOR ALL THAT INSPIRES ME.

How and when to recite this mantra: Recite this mantra three times either out loud or quietly to yourself. For added benefits, after reciting the mantra, make note of three things that inspire you. The list will help encourage you to further invite more inspiring energy into your life.

How this mantra can help you: Do you ever feel stuck in a rut? If you are looking to get inspired about your life again, this is the perfect mantra for you. Sometimes we can find ourselves going through the motions of everyday life without truly living. When this happens, it is important that you bring inspiration, joy, and passion back into your life. The words in this mantra will slowly begin to reprogram your mind so that you can make more space for the things that truly inspire you. We all have things that inspire us; the trick is to find what they are and then make the time to actually do them. To organize your thoughts, make a list of all the things that you enjoy doing. Then do at least two to three items on it every single day. This, along with practicing the mantra, will fill your life with copious amounts of inspiration and joy. When you make space for inspiration, it can uplift the energy and vibration of your entire life and bring you much more joy and happiness.

I AM EFFORTLESSLY CREATING A LIFE I LOVE.

How and when to recite this mantra: Recite this mantra six times either out loud or quietly to yourself.

How this mantra can help you: Do you love your life? If the answer is no, then it's time to make a change! You deserve to lead a life that brings you joy and makes you feel happy. You deserve to lead a life that you are in love with. In fact, true success is really about waking up and feeling joyful, healthy, and happy no matter what circumstances come your way. True success is about loving your life, no matter where you may find yourself.

It takes time to create big, long-term results using this mantra, but almost instantly it will get you thinking about ways you can love your life more. To help the process along, make a mental list of at least ten things that you love in your life now. Then, make a list of ten things that you *don't* love in your life now. Now, with the lists in front of you, ask yourself if there is a way to change the things that you don't love so they will move to the love list. If not, is there a way to learn to love them? Beyond that, try not to get too caught up in the things that are bringing your life down. Instead, bring more focus and attention to the things that make you feel good. Over time, this process will help you create more loving and positive things in your life.

I BELIEVE IN MYSELF AND KNOW I CAN DO ANYTHING.

How and when to recite this mantra: Recite this mantra three times either out loud or quietly to yourself.

How this mantra can help you: When you believe in yourself, there is nothing that you can't achieve. In fact, the only thing that is going to motivate you to achieve your goals is actually believing that you can. The words of this mantra will amplify your feelings of self-belief so that you can program your mind for success. This will give you the faith and courage you need to achieve all of your dreams, goals, and wishes.

This mantra also gives you the strength to move past whatever hurdles life sets before you and reinforces the truth that there is nothing you can't handle. Life never gives you anything that you can't handle. Use this mantra whenever you feel the voice of doubt creeping in or when you feel fearful about something in your life. Even if you don't believe in yourself 100 percent as you recite this mantra, with regular practice you very soon will. And then you will be truly unstoppable.

I HAVE EVERYTHING I NEED TO LIVE THE LIFE I DESIRE.

How and when to recite this mantra: Recite this mantra three times either out loud or quietly to yourself while placing your hands in a prayer position over your heart.

How this mantra can help you: The truth is that you already have everything you need to live the life that you desire—you just need to look within and discover this for yourself. Part of this process can be achieved through reciting this mantra, and the other part is achieved by learning who you really are. You have all the knowledge and the wisdom inside of you to create a life that feels good from the inside out. If you want to feel this on the deepest of levels, try engaging in mindfulness practices like meditation or even creative projects. They can help you to become more aware of who you are.

This mantra is also perfect to use when you find yourself living in scarcity or when you are struggling to trust the flow of your life. When you find yourself feeling fearful about the direction of your life, or if you are feeling scared or stuck in a particular situation, work with this mantra and see how it slowly begins to shift and change your mindset. Over time, this mantra will allow you to see that you have so many wonderful resources around you that you can use to get you where you want to be.

IT IS SAFE FOR ME TO MOVE OUT OF MY COMFORT ZONE IN ORDER TO GROW.

How and when to recite this mantra: Recite this mantra ten times either out loud or quietly to yourself while placing your hands over your stomach. This area contains a powerful energy center that can help you connect with your courage.

How this mantra can help you: While being in your comfort zone is great, staying too long in this space can cause your energy to stagnate. This can cause you to feel bored or despondent about your life. Spiritually, feeling despondent can cause you to lose your motivation and your zest for life. Physically, it can make you feel run-down, tired, and drained. In order to keep growing and reaching new levels in life, you have to keep pushing yourself out of your comfort zone and into new territory. Use this mantra to get excited again! Life is meant to be an adventure, and some of the best experiences are the ones you find outside of your comfort zone, not in it. Many of us fear change, but this mantra reinforces your feelings of safety so that you can release any fears you have. This mantra will also help you to feel safe and confident moving on in your life so that you can get to where you want to be.

THERE IS ALWAYS SOMETHING IN MY LIFE TO FEEL GRATEFUL FOR.

How and when to recite this mantra: Recite this mantra seven times either out loud or quietly to yourself while holding your hands in a prayer position over your heart.

How this mantra can help you: Gratitude is one of the most powerful vibrations in the Universe, and by tuning into it and really feeling it, you put yourself in a position to make positive and impactful changes in your life. After reciting this mantra, make a list of a few things that you currently feel grateful for. This can include big things that happened to you during the day or smaller things that simply brought a smile to your face. When you embrace gratitude and fill your life with it, your vibration increases. This makes you a powerful magnet for success. When you focus on all the beauty in life, life often returns the favor by showing you more beauty. This a powerful mantra that is really good to use at any time or stage of your life.

CHAPTER 6

MANTRAS FOR ABUNDANCE

These mantras will help you tune into the abundant energy of the Universe so that you can feel and experience prosperity in all areas of your life. Use these mantras to release any blocks you may have surrounding money, and rely on them in times when you don't feel worthy of receiving the many blessings that life has to offer.

abundance mantra 1

MONEY IS CONSTANTLY FLOWING INTO MY LIFE.

How and when to recite this mantra: Recite this mantra three times either out loud or quietly to yourself with your hands outstretched and palms facing up. This position of receiving will open you to the flow of abundance.

How this mantra can help you: It is easy to focus on lack and scarcity in your life, especially when it comes to money. We all have bills to pay and expenses to deal with, and sometimes this can cause us to develop a negative association with money. In fact, many people have such a negative relationship with money that they consider it to be the root of all evil. This belief is never going to help you find abundance, so it is important to shed it and, instead, find a positive relationship with money.

Through reciting this mantra, you will shift your mindset to focus on the amazing abundance that is around you right now in all areas of your life. You can be grateful for the money that *is* flowing into your life, and this gratitude can increase your awareness around the money that you do have rather than the money that you don't have. Giving thanks for the money you have turns you into a magnet for abundance. When you appreciate all that you are receiving, it is almost like the Universe rewards you by giving you more. Over time, saying this mantra and giving thanks will help money flow into your life in both miraculous and unexpected ways.

abundance mantra 2

I FEEL ABUNDANT IN ALL AREAS OF MY LIFE.

How and when to recite this mantra: Recite this mantra seven times either out loud or quietly to yourself.

How this mantra can help you: Feeling abundant means feeling supported and provided for by life and the Universe. There is more than enough abundance in this Universe for everyone, and we need not live in fear of lack or competition. Just because you receive doesn't mean someone else needs to miss out. Likewise, you will not miss out because someone else has received. If you shift your awareness for a moment, you can see that there is plenty—for example, through Mother Nature. Mother Nature always provides an abundance of everything, whether it is oxygen, sunshine, or glittering stars. We all get what we need, as long as we remember to ask for it and make sure we are aligned with receiving it.

In your own life, you can also shift your awareness so that you see the many gifts that surround you, no matter how big or small they may be. Chances are you have many, many gifts in your life. From the air in your lungs to the food in your fridge and the hot water that runs out of your taps, abundance is all around you. You are already abundant, and reciting this mantra will help you acknowledge and feel grateful for this. Over time, honoring your abundance will help you create a more fruitful and rewarding life.

I AM ALWAYS PROVIDED FOR BY THE UNIVERSE.

How and when to recite this mantra: Recite this mantra four times either out loud or quietly to yourself while placing your hands over your heart.

How this mantra can help you: It is so much easier to move through the world believing that the Universe has your back, that it is there to support you and provide for you in times of need. The more you believe this to be true, the more you will start seeing it in action for yourself. When you find yourself needing support or abundance from the Universe, recite this mantra and see how it causes a shift in your thought patterns. Believing you are supported and provided for by the Universe will motivate you to think of solutions to your problems rather than focusing on your problems. When you trust that you are being provided for by the Universe, you have the inspiration you need to keep moving forward despite the obstacles you may face.

To see that the Universe is actively supporting you, think back to a time in your life when a solution came from out of the blue or when you felt really guided or directed to follow through on something. Reflecting back on examples like these can increase your feelings of connection to the world around you and to the Divine guidance of the Universe.

EVERY DOLLAR I SPEND COMES BACK TO ME IN MIRACULOUS WAYS.

How and when to recite this mantra: Recite this mantra ten times either out loud or quietly to yourself whenever you have unexpected bills to pay or financial obligations.

How this mantra can help you: This mantra is great to use when you are feeling overwhelmed by financial obligations or are surprised by bills. Whenever you have to make a payment of some kind, whether it be a parking ticket or your groceries, believing the money will come back to you in a multitude of ways will open you up to the rhythm and flow of abundance that exists in the Universe. In order to receive abundance, you have to allow yourself to give and receive wholeheartedly. If you feel tense, angry, or frustrated when you have to give money back into the Universe, it is going to flow back to you with this same vibration. In order to welcome in the receiving of abundance, you have to welcome in the *giving* of abundance as well, and this includes paying those pesky bills or parking fines. So the next time you receive an unwanted bill, hand over the money knowing that it is going to come back to you in miraculous ways. Keep chanting this mantra on a regular basis and very soon you will begin to notice that the money you give out flows right back in.

abundance mantra 7

I ALWAYS HAVE MORE THAN ENOUGH.

How and when to recite this mantra: Recite this mantra three times either out loud or quietly to yourself.

How this mantra can help you: The Universe always gives you what you need. If you feel like you don't have enough and you want to create more, you may need to take a look at some of your beliefs and values in regard to abundance. Do you have fearful thoughts surrounding money? Do you constantly feel like you don't have enough? To get out of this mindset of lack or scarcity, you have to begin thinking abundantly, and you have to do this even if you are not seeing it in your life just yet.

Reciting this mantra will open you to abundance, and addressing any fearful thoughts will help too. If you notice any thoughts that are rooted in lack or not having enough, see if you can switch them around to something more positive. Perhaps you can simply replace those thoughts with this mantra. When you start to replace scarcity thinking with abundance thinking, you will feel far more supported by life. Soon enough, abundance will start flowing in. Knowing that you always have enough and that all your needs are being taken care of is a powerful place to live from, and this mantra will help you to get there. The more you recite this mantra, the more you will start to see that you always have enough to fulfill your needs.

abundance mantra 8

I AM BECOMING BETTER AT MANAGING MY MONEY.

How and when to recite this mantra: Recite this mantra eight times either out loud or quietly to yourself.

How this mantra can help you: Many people struggle with managing their money. They find it difficult to stay on top of their expenses and live within their means. Money management issues are often much deeper than just poor judgment—in fact, they can often signal underlying emotional issues surrounding self-worth, self-sabotage, and taking responsibility for your life.

If you are struggling to manage your money effectively, then perhaps you have some subconscious motivations or intentions behind the money decisions you are making. Are you spending money you don't have because you are trying to keep up with those around you for appearance's sake? Or are you squirreling away money and living from a place of deprivation because you fear not having enough money? Whatever the issues, the more you work on addressing them, the easier managing your money will become. As you begin this healing and learning journey in regard to money, this mantra will be there to support you. The more you recite this mantra, the more it will become a truth for you and the more confident you will feel in regard to your finances.

I LIVE IN CONTINUOUS COMFORT AND JOY.

How and when to recite this mantra: Recite this mantra five times either out loud or quietly to yourself. For added benefits, as you recite the mantra, visualize a comforting white light around your entire body.

How this mantra can help you: Part of feeling abundant is leading a life that feels fulfilling, whole, and joyous. You could chase all the money in the world, but at the end of the day, true joy and happiness are found within. This mantra is particularly useful when you are in need of an energy boost and when you are looking to create abundance in your life on a deeper, spiritual level. True abundance is how you feel about yourself and your life regardless of how much money is in your bank account. If you have been dealing with money struggles or feeling stressed about recent events in your life, this mantra is there to remind you to bring your focus back to feelings of comfort and joy. Perhaps you need to take a break from worrying and stressing and instead find ways to bring more comfort and joy into your life, even if it is just in very small ways. If you focus on creating feelings of happiness and ease now, rather than waiting until you have more money to do so, you can enter into a new and powerful vibration of peace and true abundance.

I MAKE ROOM IN MY LIFE TO RECEIVE BLESSINGS OF ABUNDANCE.

How and when to recite this mantra: Recite this mantra three times either out loud or quietly to yourself. To maximize its effectiveness, write down or recite a short intention about the blessing of abundance you would like to receive. For example, "I make room in my life to receive the blessings of a loving, romantic relationship."

How this mantra can help you: If you want to receive more abundance in your life, whether it be money, fulfillment, love, or comfort, this mantra is here to help. This mantra works in two ways. First, it opens up your energetic vibration to welcoming and receiving new blessings by setting an intention to bring these things into your life. Second, this mantra brings your awareness to all the things in your life that need to be released so that you can welcome in abundance. If you want to make changes in your life, or simply welcome in something new, you have to clear space in your existing life, on either a small or big scale. Sometimes these changes need to be on a physical level; other times you need to make emotional changes. The words in this mantra will guide you to the right action to take. You will also organically become aware of when your energy levels become spread too thin or when you become fixated on problems or dramas that are not really serving you. It's important to reserve your energetic space for the things that really matter. This shift in your attitude and energy will help your intentions to become far more powerful and will speed up the delivery of many blessings into your life.

MANTRAS FOR ABUNDANCE | 127

abundance mantra 11

I AM WORTHY OF RECEIVING ALL THAT I DESIRE.

How and when to recite this mantra: Recite this mantra three times either out loud or quietly to yourself.

How this mantra can help you: What do you really desire in your life? Chances are if you still the voices in your mind and go within, you will discover that what you truly desire is something along the lines of peace, joy, and love. These are fundamental human desires that to some extent we all crave and desire in our lives. Go deep within your own heart and see what emotions are resting there and what your true self really desires at this point in your life. By opening up to your heart's desire, you can reveal a much clearer vision for your future and what type of actions you should take moving forward.

Feeling worthy of receiving what you desire is really about boosting your levels of confidence and self-love, and knowing that part of your destiny in this life is to be able to access the true desires of your heart. You deserve to have whatever you desire in this life, as long as what you desire comes from a place of love and not ego. Sometimes our egos like to trick us into believing that we want more money, more status, more time, and so on. But material wants are transient and fleeting. They are no comparison to the true feelings of happiness that arise from within. Money can help you, but it won't make you happy, so shift your desires to be more aligned with your heart. Then, by reciting this mantra, you will begin to bring these desires into your life more and more each day.

I DESERVE TO BE WEALTHY AND PROSPEROUS IN ALL AREAS OF MY LIFE.

How and when to recite this mantra: Recite this mantra three times either out loud or quietly to yourself with your arms outstretched and palms facing up. This position will help you activate the energy of receiving.

How this mantra can help you: Many of us carry around the belief that we are not smart enough or powerful enough to be wealthy or prosperous in life. Many of us have been programmed with the belief that life needs to be a struggle and that we need to fight to get by in the world. This mentality puts your vibration into a place of scarcity and lack and closes you off from receiving the energy of abundance. To truly welcome prosperity into your life, you need to shed the beliefs that make you feel that you are not worthy of this state of being. You may need to revisit your childhood and observe your parents' relationship with money and prosperity to learn how it rubbed off on you or shaped your beliefs today. If these beliefs are not positive or are rooted in fear, consider releasing them from your life and developing new beliefs that are focused on feelings of abundance and self-worth. If you're not ready to release those beliefs just yet, even simply being aware of them is enough to get you started on changing your vibration and being a magnet for money.

I AM GRATEFUL FOR THE MANY BLESSINGS COMING MY WAY.

How and when to recite this mantra: Recite this mantra four times either out loud or quietly to yourself while placing your hands over your heart.

How this mantra can help you: Honoring and giving thanks for future blessings shifts you into a mindset of receiving. It also helps open your energy to attracting blessings into your life. There are blessings all around you, but it is your ability to receive and honor them that dictates how these blessings will flow into your life. When you are closed off or ungrateful for the blessings in your life, you create blocks; but if you are grateful for all you have received and are going to receive, blessings will flow into your life with ease and grace. Think of this like a straw placed into a glass of water. If the straw is blocked up or if there is a hole in the side of the straw, then it will be harder or even impossible for the water to move through it, even if there is a large amount of water in the glass. But if the straw is an open channel, the water will be able to move freely and abundantly through it. This metaphor is the same when it comes to receiving blessings or abundance. Just like there is plenty of water in the glass, there is also plenty of abundance around us all the time. We just have to ensure that we have a clear channel for receiving it, and reciting this mantra will help with this process.

EVERYTHING I NEED TO CREATE ABUNDANCE IS WITHIN.

How and when to recite this mantra: Recite this mantra five times either out loud or quietly to yourself.

How this mantra can help you: Many people believe that they need things outside of themselves, such as more money or more status, in order to have or create abundance in their lives. They start chasing the idea of "more" and believe that in order to feel rich or successful they need more and more stuff—the fancy car, the big house, and so on. Pursuing this type of life will forever keep you trapped in a limited mindset or a mindset that is based in fear. True abundance comes from within, and you have already been given everything you need in order to live and create an abundant life. When you understand this, it allows you to shift your perception from your external world to your internal world. It also allows you to recognize the thoughts and self-limiting beliefs that are keeping you trapped in the repetitive conditioning of your past. When you become aware of these destructive beliefs, you can then begin to replace them with positive thoughts and positive actions. This, in turn, will have profound effects on your life and will allow you to truly access abundance on the deepest of levels.

No matter what goals or blessings you want to bring into your life, all you have to do is look inside and believe that you have the strength, knowledge, and support to do so, no matter what your circumstances.

IT IS EASY FOR ME TO MAKE MORE MONEY.

How and when to recite this mantra: Recite this mantra three times either out loud or quietly to yourself.

How this mantra can help you: This mantra will help you reprogram your beliefs surrounding your ability to make more money. Many of us feel that earning money takes hard work and lots of effort, but it doesn't have to feel like that. In fact, feeling this way is a belief that can be easily changed if you use this mantra and the power of your mind. Just like you have programmed yourself to believe that making money is hard, you have the ability to reprogram yourself to believe that making money is effortless and easy. Reshaping your mind to accept this powerful belief will give you more energy and stamina to come up with creative ideas for how to bring more money into your life. In fact, over time you will start to see with your own eyes how easy it can be to bring money into your life. This mantra is perfect to use if you feel stressed about money or if you find it hard to make ends meet. By chanting these words on a regular basis, you will begin to feel more relaxed about money and, in turn, more money will begin to flow into your life with less effort and far more abundance.

abundance mantra 16

I ALLOW MYSELF TO ENJOY ALL THE GOOD THINGS IN LIFE.

How and when to recite this mantra: Recite this mantra three times either out loud or quietly to yourself. After reciting the mantra, take three breaths in and out, close your eyes, and reflect on something that brings you joy in your life.

How this mantra can help you: How often do you remind yourself to stop and actually enjoy life? This mantra is designed to help you bring your awareness to all the fun, laughter, and prosperity in your life so that you can actually enjoy yourself and your life on earth. You only get one shot at life, so you may as well make the most of it and do everything you can to ensure that it is a happy, fun, and positive one. Many of us get caught up in our lives, moving from day to day without really living to the fullest of our potential. This mantra is here to remind you that part of your purpose in this life is learning to enjoy yourself and find the fun even in mundane tasks. Instead of getting swept up by life and trying to "solve" everything, this mantra reminds you to focus on seeing the good in everything and everyone. By taking this approach to life, you can help yourself feel a lot more relaxed and lighthearted about the things that unfold.

I AM OPEN TO NEW SOURCES OF WEALTH.

How and when to recite this mantra: Recite this mantra three times either out loud or quietly to yourself.

How this mantra can help you: Wealth comes from many avenues and is not just related to your income. You can feel wealthy in knowledge, wealthy in health, and wealthy in joy. This mantra is effective for bringing wealth and abundance into your life from all angles and for creating feelings of fulfillment and happiness. Feeling abundant regardless of your circumstances is a powerful place to live from and can help you feel prosperous and fulfilled. Sometimes the greatest wealth can even be found in the most unsuspecting places and in the most unexpected ways. Simply giving a smile, cheering up someone else, or performing a small act of charity can bring waves of abundant and wealthy feelings into your life. There are so many ways to embrace wealth in life, and this mantra is perfect if you want to infuse your life with this magical energy.

MY WORTH IS NOT DEPENDENT ON MY FINANCIAL SITUATION.

How and when to recite this mantra: Recite this mantra three times either out loud or quietly to yourself.

How this mantra can help you: How much value do you put on money? Many of us believe that the more money we have, the worthier we are and the more important we are. But this is a false belief. Your financial situation has nothing to do with your true worth. Rather, your true worth is dependent on how you feel about yourself. The good news is that you can control how you choose to feel about yourself. If you believe you are worthy, you will be. Just the same, if you believe you are unworthy, you will be. You may have to overcome a lifetime of social conditioning to recognize these truths.

Over time, this mantra will help to reprogram your beliefs so that you are no longer measuring your self-worth by your income. This will free you up to see yourself in a more positive and loving light. Once you feel more confident and fulfilled, you can create true and lasting happiness within yourself. When you feel good about yourself from within, regardless of what is happening on the outside, that is when you will find true, eternal happiness.

CHAPTER 7

MANTRAS TO TRANSFORM YOUR LIFE

These mantras are designed to help guide you through periods of transformation and change in your life. Use these mantras when you need comfort or inspiration to make productive and proactive changes in your life.

IT IS SAFE FOR ME TO RELEASE THE PAST; IT IS SAFE FOR ME TO MOVE ON.

How and when to recite this mantra: Recite this mantra seven times either out loud or quietly to yourself.

How this mantra can help you: Until you have released the past, you will constantly find yourself coming up against roadblocks, or you might keep repeating the same mistakes again and again. By releasing the past you can let go of the things that are holding you back. Once freed, you can welcome in new energy and begin to move forward. This mantra is perfect to use when you find yourself in a repetitive cycle or when you find yourself holding on to thoughts, memories, or visions from your past. In time, this mantra will instill belief and courage so that you can feel safe to release the burdens or thoughts of your past. No longer will you need to revisit the past and no longer will you feel scared to let go of the memories of your past. This will put you in a powerful position where you can move forward in your life without getting stuck or without feeling guilty for your past actions. Your past need not define you, and this mantra will help you to take action so that you can free yourself from the definitions you have given yourself.

I WELCOME IN A NEW BEGINNING.

How and when to recite this mantra: Recite this mantra three times out loud while standing. As you say the words, stretch your arms up and over your head like you are welcoming in the new energy of your life.

How this mantra can help you: New beginnings are always unfolding in life, and they are an exciting time of change, growth, and transformation. Sometimes we choose new beginnings, and other times we have no choice but to accept them. No matter what situation you find yourself in, try to welcome a new beginning with open arms. You will feel empowered to find your courage and strength no matter what is unfolding around you. New beginnings can seem rocky or scary at first, but once you have gotten the hang of things, starting a new chapter in your life can be extremely rewarding and fulfilling. This mantra is also perfect to use if you are ready to start a new chapter in your life but are unsure of what changes actually need to take place. By reciting this mantra, you can learn to trust that all will be revealed to you in perfect timing and that you will receive a clear understanding of what new beginnings await you.

I AM PROUD OF MYSELF FOR THE PROGRESS I HAVE MADE.

How and when to recite this mantra: Recite this mantra three times either out loud or quietly to yourself while placing your hands in a prayer position over your heart.

How this mantra can help you: When was the last time you felt proud of yourself? Chances are, you have had to endure many obstacles and setbacks to get where you are today. Be proud of your accomplishments and congratulate yourself for making it this far. When you acknowledge yourself in this way, it not only boosts your feelings of self-esteem, but it also allows you to give thanks to your mind, body, heart, and soul for getting you where you are today.

When you honor the progress you have made, it serves as a reminder that you are achieving your goals and that you are moving forward at your own pace. Very often, we can be too hard on ourselves and expect too much—we can even make ourselves feel guilty for not doing enough or not achieving our dreams faster. We all experience periods in our lives when progress feels repetitive, slow, or even nonexistent, but it's important to be patient and know that good things are ahead in your future. This knowledge will lift your mood and your energy, and it will give you more motivation to move ahead in your own time. Even if it doesn't feel like it, you are always making progress. Sometimes progress happens in exciting leaps and bounds, and sometimes it happens in the quiet, inner moments that stir from within...but either way, you are always progressing.

Transformation mantra 4

I TRUST THAT THE UNIVERSE WILL GUIDE ME TO CLARITY.

How and when to recite this mantra: Recite this mantra nine times either out loud or quietly to yourself.

How this mantra can help you: When going through a period of transformation, it can be hard to know what the road ahead may look like and where you are going to land. This fear of the unknown is very real, yet it is an important place to venture to every now and again because it helps you to grow and it helps you to get clear about what is truly important. Feeling confused about what direction to take in life is a clear sign that growth and change are in the works. Think about it: If you always felt certain about every move and every situation in your life, how would you ever really grow? How would you ever be challenged to take a risk or try something new? All confusion eventually becomes clear in time, and this mantra will help you along with that process toward clarity. By trusting that you will find clarity, and trusting that there is a plan for you, you can move through this period of uncertainty with grace and ease. The words in this mantra will help you stay in the present moment, trust your intuition, and take things one day at a time.

EVERYTHING I NEED TO KNOW IS BEING REVEALED TO ME IN PERFECT TIMING.

How and when to recite this mantra: Recite this mantra three times either out loud or quietly to yourself.

How this mantra can help you: It is common to feel uncertain about your life, people, events, and situations. It is also common to feel overwhelmed when you are trying to make a decision in your life but are lacking all the information you feel you need. Whenever this happens, you have to be patient and trust that you will be guided when the time is right. This mantra calms your mind in periods of uncertainty and instills trust that everything you need to know will be revealed when the time is perfect. If you feel stuck, sometimes it is because you are meant to be stuck in that moment. Perhaps there are things you need to learn where you currently stand, or perhaps there is unfinished business that needs attending to. Perhaps you just need to slow down and take more time to process where you are before moving forward. Regardless of your situation, this mantra will help to provide you with ease and comfort as it assures you that, in the right time, everything will be revealed. This mantra will also help evoke feelings of patience when you are anticipating new information or are waiting to hear back about an important event or discovery. The more you recite this mantra, the more at peace you will feel and the more directed you will become.

TRANSFORMATION MANTRA 6

CHANGE IS HOW I GROW.

How and when to recite this mantra: Recite this mantra ten times either out loud or quietly to yourself. For added benefits, place your hands in a prayer position over your heart as you recite the mantra.

How this mantra can help you: It can be hard to accept changes when they arrive, but it is important to remember that all changes are a sign of growth to a better and higher place—a place of strength, wisdom, and gratitude. It may not always seem that way at first, but significant life changes often can be the best and most rewarding things that happen to us in life. If you always stayed in the same place and never changed, you would never grow and you would never really be able to experience life to the fullest. Part of what we all signed up for when our souls came to earth was the adventure of life's ups and downs. So, no matter whether the changes around you are welcomed or not, it is important to embrace them and honor them for what they are, even if they don't make sense to you just yet. The only thing that is inevitable in this life is change, and reciting this mantra will help you find the purpose and peace behind whatever transitions come your way.

I USE LOVE TO MAKE ALL THE DECISIONS IN MY LIFE.

How and when to recite this mantra: This mantra is best recited after or during meditation. You can incorporate it into your own practice, or you can use the following instructions as your guide: Take three to four deep breaths in and out while placing your hand over your heart. Chant the mantra in your mind eleven times. Once finished, end your meditation by taking three to four deep breaths.

How this mantra can help you: Are the decisions you are making in life driven by fear or by love? This mantra is there to remind you to make all of the decisions in your life from a place of love rather than a place of fear. When you are facing many changes in your life, or when you are looking to transform your life to that next level, it is important to pay attention to where your intentions and actions are coming from. Most of us want to create a loving life, but many of us are making decisions from a place of fear, and doing this rarely leads us to where we want to be. When you make decisions based on love, you will be enveloped in positivity and will automatically be aligned with your highest path. To work out how to act from a place of love, you have to first silence your thoughts and tune into the quiet whisper of your heart. Reciting this mantra along with meditation practice can help you hear this whisper. Acting from your heart will lead you to respond to yourself and others from the most loving, compassionate place you can. After working with this mantra for a few weeks, you will be able to make decisions from a place of love with confidence, and this will truly transform your life.

Transformation mantra 8

I AM READY TO MAKE CHANGES IN MY LIFE THAT ARE FOR MY HIGHEST GOOD.

How and when to recite this mantra: Recite this mantra five times either out loud or quietly to yourself. Between each repetition, close your eyes and take a deep breath in and out to activate a feeling of stillness and strength.

How this mantra can help you: Every so often we need to change and upgrade our lives in different ways. Sometimes the changes we need to make are small and subtle, and other times they are much larger and transformative. This mantra prepares you to feel ready for any changes that are on the horizon. When you embrace change, life becomes far less stressful and far more enjoyable. In fact, if you learn to ride change, it can become an exciting adventure full of new opportunities! This mantra will not only prepare you for change, but it will also help you shift your mindset so that you can see the benefits in change. When you believe that changes are always happening for your highest good, then you will focus on the positive and see things from a more optimistic place. This mantra is also great to use when you find yourself stuck in a rut. Even if you don't know the right course of action that you need to take to move forward, this mantra will help prepare you for it so that the perfect answers are revealed to you at exactly the right time.

I AM FEELING MORE CERTAIN OF AND CONFIDENT IN MY PATH EVERY SINGLE DAY.

How and when to recite this mantra: Recite this mantra six times either out loud or quietly to yourself. For added benefits, gently nod as you are repeating this mantra. Nodding is a positive action that helps to affirm what you are saying.

How this mantra can help you: Being in a place of uncertainty in life can trigger feelings of anxiety, stress, and fear. When you feel confident in life, however, you feel motivated, guided, and on track with your purpose. This mantra is designed to help instill feelings of certainty and confidence in your life so that you can move forward with ease. Even if you are feeling confused about your path ahead, focusing on all the things that you feel certain about can help you shift your vibration to a powerful place of direction. Reciting this mantra can help with this process and will build up your feelings of confidence day by day. The more you focus on your confusion, the more confused you will become; but if you shift your awareness to focus on all the things you feel certain about, eventually more certainty will follow. Sometimes the only way you are going to feel certain in your life is by feeling certain within yourself. This mantra will encourage you to reflect on your own feelings of certainty and confidence. The more you reflect on these things, the easier it will be for you to make the changes you need to live the life you truly desire.

Transformation mantra 10

THE NEXT PERFECT STEP IS ALWAYS BEING REVEALED TO ME.

How and when to recite this mantra: Recite this mantra three times either out loud or quietly to yourself with your hands in a prayer position.

How this mantra can help you: As the spiritual author Eckhart Tolle states in his book *A New Earth,* "Life is the dancer and you are the dance." You are an active participant not just in your own life but in the life around you as well. As you recite this mantra and become aware of this fact, you will see that the Universe is always sending you signs guiding you forward. Sometimes the signs can simply be feelings, and other times they play out in your environment in mysterious ways. The perfect next step is always being revealed to you, and when you open yourself to this possibility, you will always feel yourself being guided in the right way at the right time. Taking a walk in nature can also open you up to the idea that the world around you is always sending you signs and clues. If you observe nature, you will see that everything is in harmony and everything is in perfect order. There is a perfection that exists in nature, and this same perfection lives with you and around you; all you need to do is trust in it. This mantra can help you become more aware of this fact, and by reciting it regularly, you will feel guided to the next perfect step when it arrives.

I AM ON THE RIGHT PATH.

How and when to recite this mantra: Recite this mantra three times either out loud or quietly to yourself.

How this mantra can help you: In truth, there is no such thing as the "right" or "wrong" path. All paths lead you to where you need to be, which means that even though every path is different, they are all perfect for you. Whatever choices you have made in life have led you to where you are now, and where you are now is exactly where you need to be. When you learn to embrace this truth you will shed any fears you may have of choosing the wrong path or making the wrong decision. Good or bad, every experience that unfolds in your life is always pushing you to a higher, more evolved, and wiser place. This mantra is there to remind you that you are always on the right path for you, and that you have the power to make changes whenever you desire. If you are unhappy with the path you are walking, you always have the power to make changes no matter how difficult it may seem. Simply tune into how you feel and follow the direction of what inspires you and makes you feel good. If you use your feelings as a compass, they will always guide you to feeling right about the direction of your life.

I SURRENDER AND RELEASE MY WORRIES TO THE UNIVERSE.

How and when to recite this mantra: Recite this mantra seven times either out loud or quietly to yourself. For added benefits, as you recite the mantra put your hands together and then on the word *release* open your arms up like you are flinging your worries out of your body and into the Universe, where they can be taken care of for you.

How this mantra can help you: You do not need to carry your burdens and worries by yourself. In fact, if you give yourself permission to release them to the Universe, you will find that in time they will take care of themselves. This is not about ditching your responsibility for your life, but it is about knowing that you have the ability to release your worries to a higher power. Many of us are under the impression that we are alone in this life, but with a shift in awareness, we can see that there are many forces beyond us that are rooting for us and our well-being. It takes faith and trust to see the world this way, and by reciting this mantra you will start to see this in action. By surrendering your worries to the Universe, you will instantly feel calmer, more relaxed, and more supported wherever you are on your journey. Over time, this can transform your life and allow you to feel far more at peace and far more guided by the Universe. To aid with this process, you can even ask the Universe to send you a sign of some kind. The Universe is always delivering signs for us to follow—such as receiving a gut feeling or experiencing synchronicities. The trick is to become open and aware enough to see them.

I AM READY TO RELEASE THE OLD SO THAT I MAY WELCOME IN THE NEW.

How and when to recite this mantra: Recite this mantra nine times either out loud or quietly to yourself.

How this mantra can help you: There comes a point in life when we have to release the old in order to make way for the new. This is something all of us must do in this life, and the more we can embrace this process, the easier it will be. In fact, the more we work on releasing the things that no longer serve us, the happier and more fulfilled we will feel. When we carry around things past their "due date," our lives can feel stagnant and uncomfortable. Just like we throw food away when it is expired, so too must we discard the junk in our lives. We must do more than purge stale situations like jobs, relationships, friendships, and so on. We must also let go of our old beliefs and even the material things that we have collected along the way. Every now and again it becomes necessary to purge your life of the old and spring clean your insides and outsides. This process can be extremely therapeutic, and it always opens the door for you to welcome in new vibrations and positive experiences. This mantra is also great to recite as you spring clean your home and get rid of all the clutter and junk that you have been collecting over the years. Objects can hold their own energy, so it is important every once in a while to do a thorough cleansing or purging in your home in order to clear out any unwanted or old energy.

I AM TRANSFORMING MY MIND AND BODY IN MIRACULOUS WAYS.

How and when to recite this mantra: Recite this mantra three times either out loud or quietly to yourself.

How this mantra can help you: This mantra is perfect to use if you are on a new diet or if you have made the decision to make positive changes to your lifestyle or thought processes. Taking this type of ownership of your life is extremely powerful and also extremely healing. In fact, when you take responsibility for changing your mind or body, the effects often trickle down into other areas of your life and can bring about many miraculous and inspired changes. The vibration of this mantra will also help you have patience with the process and will remind you to be gentle with yourself. Just as the caterpillar takes time to evolve into a butterfly, you also need time to transform. Trust in the process and know that this mantra is there to help and support you as you shift your life from the inside out. This mantra is also perfect to use when you can feel transformation in the works but are unsure of exactly how it is all going to unfold. Whenever you are in a transition period of any kind, say this mantra to help provide a level of comfort and also open up your awareness so that you can notice any changes when they arrive.

I AM FREE OF MY PAST; I AM FREE OF THE PAIN; I AM NOW FREE TO BE ME.

How and when to recite this mantra: Recite this mantra five times either out loud or quietly to yourself.

How this mantra can help you: This mantra is extremely powerful, and it works on many levels to help you reach a place of peace and fulfillment wherever you are in life. This mantra is designed to help you release past pains you may be carrying around. We all have traumas from our past, and we might be carrying guilt, sorrow, or resentment. Regardless, it is necessary to release them so that we can feel free and liberated to move on with our lives. Burying these emotions within actually causes you to relive the pain again and again. Only after you have cleaned out your pains of the past can you truly be free. Even though this may seem like a huge task, the good news is that you can start straight away by using this mantra. By reciting this mantra the recommended number of times on a daily basis, you can start to bring awareness to all the things you need to release. And once you begin to release them, you can start to find freedom in your life. The important thing to remember with this mantra is that you don't have to wait till you have released the past in order to start feeling free in your life.

I FIND THE PEACE WITHIN NO MATTER WHAT IS HAPPENING AROUND ME.

How and when to recite this mantra: Recite this mantra ten times either out loud or quietly to yourself as you place your hands in a prayer position over your heart.

How this mantra can help you: One of the most powerful things you can do is learn how to find peace and stillness during difficult moments. If you can remain calm and centered in volatile situations, you will be able to respond with compassion, love, and grace. In addition, you will know the best course of action moving forward. Finding calm and peace can be challenging to do every single time, but this mantra is here to help. It can remind you to stay grounded and still when there is chaos or destruction around you. When you find your peace and stillness in difficult situations, you actually reduce the influence they have in your life. What's more, through the clarity of calm, you will be able to see all situations from a place of distance rather than from the messy center of it all. When you do this, your energy actually becomes a repellent for drama, and you may even find that dramatic people or situations naturally melt away from your life. When you practice peace, your outer world reflects that by bringing you more peace.

I ACCEPT THIS MOMENT AND KNOW ONLY GOOD CAN COME FROM IT.

How and when to recite this mantra: Recite this mantra three times either out loud or quietly to yourself.

How this mantra can help you: It can be challenging to accept whatever comes your way, especially if what has come your way is a loss, a hardship, or a situation filled with grief. As hard as it may be, when you accept whatever flows into your life, you will relax and see things from a broader perspective. In fact, sometimes when you accept what comes your way, you can find solutions where you might otherwise see only problems. Acceptance also allows you to focus on what you can do to improve the situation and deemphasize what has gone wrong. Even if you can't fix the situation completely, chances are there are many things you can do to make yourself feel better or to ease the stress or grief associated with it. By bringing your attention to the solution rather than resisting the situation, you can help the good in the situation to emerge. There is always a silver lining, and even though we sometimes need more time or patience to realize this, we can speed this process along through acceptance.

EVERYTHING UNFOLDING NOW IS HELPING ME TO REALIZE MY TRUE POWER AND POTENTIAL.

How and when to recite this mantra: Recite this mantra three times either out loud or quietly to yourself.

How this mantra can help you: Everything that is unfolding in your life now exists to teach you something so that you can grow stronger, wiser, and more enlightened. This is the path that we are all walking in this life, and this mantra is here to remind you of this. Whatever comes your way exists to help you realize the true power and potential that lives inside of you. If you embrace every challenge in your life as an opportunity to shine, as an opportunity to know yourself better, then you will always be able to understand the higher purpose that life holds. Reciting this mantra will help you shift your vibration to a place of positivity and power so that you can view everything in your life from a place of pure understanding. We are all climbing our own mountains, and sometimes there is rugged terrain ahead and sometimes there is smooth terrain ahead, but both of these experiences are there to teach you and inspire you so you can do the same for others. Recite this mantra when you are dealing with challenges or when you are enveloped in bliss, for it will always bring you a new level of understanding.

THERE ARE NO LIMITS ON WHO I CAN BECOME.

How and when to recite this mantra: Recite this mantra three times either out loud or quietly to yourself for instant inspiration and motivation.

How this mantra can help you: There are no limits on what you can achieve and who you can become in this life. In fact, the only limits are the ones you put on yourself. Many of us carry around limiting beliefs about our abilities, our appearance, and our potential. These beliefs can block you from achieving your dreams and getting you to where you want to be, so it is important to become aware of them and replace them with some new beliefs whenever possible. This mantra can help you to shed those self-limiting beliefs by shedding light on them. From this place of insight, you can change them into something more positive. Reciting this mantra gives you the confidence you need to step out of your comfort zone and go after your highest dreams and wishes. The sky is truly the limit, and this mantra will remind you of that.

CHAPTER 8
MANTRAS FOR BEDTIME

These mantras are designed to put you in a relaxed, calm, and peaceful state so you can fall asleep easily and sleep deeply. Use these mantras as an evening meditation to help wind down for the day, reflect on the day gone by, and settle your mind for a peaceful night of sweet dreaming.

I AM BLESSED AND GRATEFUL FOR ALL I LEARNED TODAY.

How and when to recite this mantra: Recite this mantra three times either out loud or quietly to yourself with your hands in a prayer position.

How this mantra can help you: You have the power to see everything that comes your way as either a blessing or a curse. While this choice is always yours, it definitely makes life easier when you choose to see everything as a blessing—even if it is a blessing in disguise! By reflecting on your day and focusing on the blessings that it brought your way, you not only relax and settle your mind for sleep, but you also develop a positive mindset about your life in general. Seeing everything as a lesson also helps evoke this feeling and will remind you that even though life is a journey of ups and downs, there is so much to be grateful for. Whether it's the beautiful sunset, your family and friends, the delicious meal you had for dinner, or the roof over your head, chances are that your life is filled with an abundance of blessings. Reciting this mantra before bed will also help you focus on the wonderful things that happened so that you are not tossing and turning with stress as you try to fall asleep.

I CLEAR MY MIND OF ANY THOUGHTS AND GIVE MYSELF PERMISSION TO REST.

How and when to recite this mantra: Recite this mantra five times either out loud or quietly to yourself just before bed. You can also recite this mantra in your mind as you are falling asleep. If you are still struggling to fall asleep, you can practice a journaling exercise. Simply write down everything you are thinking and feeling so it is out on paper and not in your mind. Often, giving your thoughts an outlet helps to calm your mind and prepare you for sleep. After the journaling exercise, you can then recite the mantra as you fall asleep.

How this mantra can help you: One of the main reasons people struggle with falling asleep is that their minds are racing a million miles per hour with an abundance of thoughts. Often, when you take the time to clear your thoughts, you make it much easier to fall asleep. By reciting this mantra, you naturally clear the clutter from your mind and shift your mindset to a place of rest and relaxation. All of your problems, issues, and worries can wait while you take this time for yourself. This simple belief can not only help you fall asleep, but it also reminds you of the importance of looking after yourself. If you are still struggling to calm your thoughts, you can practice a simple visualization exercise where you see yourself going for a walk along the beach or through a forest. As you visualize yourself walking down the path, keep chanting the mantra while observing all of the other relaxing sights and sounds. After doing this for just a few minutes, chances are you will be fast asleep.

IT IS EASY FOR ME TO FALL ASLEEP.

How and when to recite this mantra: Recite this mantra in your mind as many times as needed as you drift off to sleep.

How this mantra can help you: Part of what makes mantras so successful is that they reprogram beliefs that you have held about yourself. This reprogramming can actually support the healing process for conditions like insomnia. By reciting this mantra, you help reprogram the belief that falling asleep is difficult for you or that you can't fall asleep as easily as you would like. It is amazing how our beliefs can shape our lives, so if you are dealing with insomnia, or if you struggle to fall asleep, this mantra may be just what you need to bring a shift in your beliefs so that you can change your sleeping habits. After all, what we believe about ourselves generally becomes our truth. While reciting this mantra may not be the ultimate cure, it will help you approach sleep from a healthier and more positive mindset. For best results, use this mantra on a nightly basis for at least thirty days. Over this time period you may begin to notice subtle changes to your sleeping routine, and you may even find that falling asleep happens a lot easier.

AS I BREATHE I FEEL MYSELF DRIFTING OFF INTO A DEEP SLEEP.

How and when to recite this mantra: Recite this mantra seven times in your mind while taking deep breaths in and out. You can also alternate between reciting the mantra and taking deep breaths.

How this mantra can help you: Focusing on your breath is a great way to relax your body and still your mind. In fact, the breath can be one of the most powerful tools when it comes to settling your energy for a peaceful night of sleep. Reciting this mantra allows you to feel the rhythm and power of your breath so that you can become relaxed, calm, and ready for sleep. This mantra is also perfect to use when you find yourself going over events of the day or thinking about all the things that you need to do tomorrow. Replacing all of your thoughts with the repetition of this mantra can help you to drift off into a deep and peaceful night of sleep. If you are still struggling to fall asleep, simply concentrating on your breath can also help. Take slow inhales and exhales for at least a minute or two. This simple practice helps calm your mind and induces feelings of sleepiness.

MY GUARDIAN ANGELS WATCH OVER ME AND REFRESH MY SPIRIT AS I SLEEP.

How and when to recite this mantra: Recite this mantra three times just before bed either out loud or quietly to yourself. For added benefits, visualize a protective white light surrounding your body as you recite this mantra.

How this mantra can help you: We all have guardian angels who protect and guide us through life. This mantra invites your guardian angels to watch over you while you sleep so that you can feel safe, comforted, and secure through the night. This can be an extremely comforting thought, especially if you suffer from nightmares, night terrors, sleep paralysis, or anxiety at night. This mantra not only invites your angels to protect you while you sleep, but it also invites them to recharge and restore your energy so that you can wake up feeling refreshed and energetic in the morning. Who doesn't want that? Use this mantra whenever you are feeling unsettled about going to sleep. It can help you find calm and ease sleep-related fears that may be swimming around in your head. After reciting this mantra, you should begin to feel more relaxed and peaceful almost immediately.

AS I SLEEP, I RESTORE THE HEALTH AND WELL-BEING OF MY BODY, MIND, AND SOUL.

How and when to recite this mantra: Recite this mantra three times either out loud or quietly to yourself before bed while placing your right hand over your heart and your left hand over your stomach. These are powerful energy centers of the body that are restored while you sleep.

How this mantra can help you: We all know how good it feels to get a great night of sleep. Sleeping well gives us the energy and motivation we need to get through the day, and it makes it easier for us to see the positive in every situation. This mantra acts as a bedtime prayer that can be said to evoke a healing and restorative night of sleep. Through reciting this mantra, you are setting an intention of what you would like to get out of your sleep. When used over time, your body and mind will start to respond. This mantra is also great to use when you are looking to aid the healing process of any disease, illness, or emotional trauma while you sleep. While you sleep, your body, mind, and emotions are all being refreshed. And by chanting this mantra before bedtime, you can set a more deliberate intention for this healing to occur. Practice using this mantra for a few weeks. Over time, you may begin to wake up feeling completely reborn.

I RELEASE THE EVENTS OF THE DAY AND FORGIVE MYSELF AND OTHERS.

How and when to recite this mantra: Recite this mantra three times either out loud or quietly to yourself just before bed. To aid in the releasing process, you can write down any events of the day that are preying on your mind before reciting this mantra.

How this mantra can help you: It is very important to clear the events of the day. When you hold on to events and replay them in your mind, you not only make it more difficult to fall asleep, but you also create stagnant energy that can eventually create blocks in your life. This mantra is designed to help you both release the energy of the day gone by and forgive yourself and others for any mistakes, mishaps, or hardships that occurred. Forgiving yourself and others is extremely healing and liberating, and doing so can help you release any negative or pent-up emotions. If you like, you can keep a journal by your bedside to write down any thoughts that you need to release and forgive yourself or others for. If you can get in the habit of releasing and forgiving the day, you can both sleep more peacefully and clear your energy so that you are ready for an even better tomorrow.

MY BODY IS LIGHT; MY MIND IS QUIET; I FEEL COMPLETELY RELAXED.

How and when to recite this mantra: Recite this mantra three times either out loud or quietly to yourself just before bed. For added benefits, take three deep breaths in and out between each repetition.

How this mantra can help you: This mantra is designed to put you in the perfect mindset for falling asleep. In order to fall asleep your body has to completely relax and surrender. Many people find it hard to relax and surrender to this level, which is why many suffer from poor sleeping patterns. We all know how important it is to get a good night of sleep, and this mantra is here to help program your mind to achieve just that. By reciting this mantra before bed, you can help shift yourself into a state of relaxation and lightness. This feeling will help you drift off to sleep a lot more easily and will help you stay asleep throughout the night. If you find it hard to let go and relax, this mantra is the perfect remedy. Over time, you will start to notice a shift in your sleeping habits and bedtime behavior. For added benefits, take deep and relaxing breaths as you recite this mantra. Focusing on your breath can help you evoke feelings of peace and relaxation.

I GIVE THANKS FOR THIS BEAUTIFUL DAY AND KNOW THAT TOMORROW WILL BE EVEN BETTER.

How and when to recite this mantra: Recite this mantra either out loud or quietly to yourself just before bed.

How this mantra can help you: Feeling grateful for the day gone by is a powerful way to honor yourself, your life, and the Universe. When you give thanks for what you have, the Universe always blesses you with more. Gratitude can also raise your feelings of happiness and allow you to focus on all the good that is in your life. This mantra is designed to help evoke positive and uplifting feelings so that you can go to bed feeling relaxed and excited about tomorrow. This mantra can stir up feelings of anticipation about the future and can get your mind focused on all the wonderful things that will be waiting for you in the morning. Tomorrow really is a new day and we should all be excited about what opportunities it holds. Waking up each day is truly a gift that many of us take for granted, but this mantra will allow you to tune into the amazing blessing of life and get you looking forward to whatever tomorrow may bring your way.

IT IS SAFE FOR ME TO FALL ASLEEP, FOR I KNOW ALL IS WELL.

How and when to recite this mantra: Recite this mantra three times either out loud or quietly to yourself just before bed.

How this mantra can help you: It can be hard to fall asleep when there are unsolved problems, arguments, or situations in your life. Sometimes you can toss and turn all night thinking and thinking and even thinking some more! In order to avoid this, and to get a restful night of sleep, use this mantra to instill the feeling that all is well. Getting a good night of sleep can often help you to see a problem so much more clearly in the morning. Some time, distance, and a restful night of slumber can work wonders, and this mantra is perfect to use whenever overwhelming thoughts are blocking you from relaxing, turning off, and going to sleep. Although your problems might still be there waiting for you in the morning, when you wake up with a fresh mindset and a clear perspective, the answers and solutions you need may just be a whole lot easier to find. Use this mantra whenever you need reassurance before bedtime. The soothing words and the reminder that "all is well" will help you relax so that you can tackle things head-on in the morning.

I AM CALM; I AM STILL; I AM DIVINE.

How and when to recite this mantra: Recite this mantra either out loud or quietly to yourself with your hands in a prayer position over your heart. This mantra is best used before bed but can also be used whenever needed.

How this mantra can help you: This powerful, heartwarming mantra is designed to help evoke feelings of peace and tranquillity so you can have a restful night of sleep. By reciting this mantra, you will feel more relaxed and centered so that you can tune into the inner stirrings of your heart. It is only when your mind is still and quiet that you can really tap into your true essence and feel the Divine energy that flows from your heart and all around you. When you tune into this Divine essence, you are reminded of your strength and power, and you are also reminded how much you are loved. This mantra is perfect to use when you are looking to develop a stronger connection with your inner self or to connect to the Divine energy that flows from within. We all have Divine energy within us, and when you still your mind and tune into the gentle hum of your heart, you will be able to feel it.

I AM CONTENT AND SATISFIED WITH EVERYTHING I ACCOMPLISHED TODAY.

How and when to recite this mantra: Recite this mantra three times either out loud or quietly to yourself as you are winding down for the day.

How this mantra can help you: Sometimes it can be hard to turn off at night, especially when you have lots on your plate or you lead a busy lifestyle. This mantra is designed to evoke feelings of contentment with what you have achieved during the day. If you are upset because you did not complete everything that you wished to, this mantra can help you have patience, acceptance, and understanding. It is not always possible to do everything, especially in one day, and this mantra reminds you to be gentle with yourself. Instead of beating yourself up for the things you didn't do, you should celebrate what you did do. Tomorrow truly is another day, and it holds the opportunity for a fresh start and a new beginning. This mantra helps you achieve a powerful mindset shift that will not only reduce your feelings of stress but will also make you more productive in the long term. By stating that you are satisfied with all you did, you allow yourself to feel a sense of accomplishment. Over time, this can boost your feelings of self-worth and self-esteem.

LET IT BE.

How and when to recite this mantra: Recite this mantra three times slowly either out loud or quietly to yourself just before bed.

How this mantra can help you: This mantra is simple yet powerful. It serves as a reminder that you don't need to have everything sorted out perfectly before you go to sleep. Tomorrow is a new day, and tomorrow always brings new opportunities and new possibilities that you perhaps didn't see or know about before. By reciting this mantra, you will be reminded to allow things to be as they are, for tomorrow will be another day and another chance will present itself for you to do things differently. As you fall asleep, reminding yourself to let things be as they are can help you relax and settle in for a night of deep sleep. As much as we sometimes want to, we cannot do everything in a day, and sometimes it is not even our job to do everything. This mantra serves as a powerful reminder that you should allow things to be as they are without worrying or stressing about it. Everything will get done in perfect timing and as it needs to be done, so just let it be.

BEDTIME mantra 14

I AM OPEN TO RECEIVING INTUITIVE MESSAGES THROUGH MY DREAMS.

How and when to recite this mantra: Recite this mantra nine times either out loud or quietly to yourself just before bed.

How this mantra can help you: By setting your intention before bed, you increase your awareness in regard to your dreams and the messages they have for you. It has long been believed that dreams offer glimpses into our deeper subconscious thoughts. Indeed, we can receive inspiration, insights, and even intuitive messages through our dreams. Although the meaning of our dreams may not always be clear-cut, often the feeling that the dream evokes can point us in the direction of what may be going on beneath the surface. By paying attention to your dreams, you can not only learn more about yourself, but you can also start flexing your intuitive muscles. Over time, this mantra can help you to become more aware of your dreams so that you can remember them better and interpret them better. For added benefits, you can keep a dream journal by your bedside. You can use it to record all of your dreams first thing in the morning. This will not only help you to remember them, but it will also give you the opportunity to look back through your dreams and interpret any themes or messages that seem to be unfolding.

ALL MY PROBLEMS MELT AWAY AS I DRIFT OFF TO SLEEP.

How and when to recite this mantra: Recite this mantra three times either out loud or quietly to yourself just before bed. For added benefits, visualize your problems melting away in the form of a heavy weight or coat that is being released from your shoulders.

How this mantra can help you: We all know how things can seem clearer in the morning, which is why this mantra can be so effective. Sometimes after getting a solid night of rest, your problems of yesterday seem more manageable and can be figured out much more easily. This mantra will help you release any pent-up emotions, thoughts, or energy around what has happened during the day so that you can relax and get some sleep. By visualizing your problems melting away, you will also feel lighter and less burdened by whatever dramas unfolded. For added benefits, you can visualize your problems melting away by using your breath. Every time you exhale, visualize your problems leaving with the breath. Then, as you inhale, visualize yourself breathing in a calming, relaxing energy to replace the problems. This simple breath work increases the potency of the mantra and will have you drifting off to the land of wink and nod in no time.

AS I FALL ASLEEP, I FOCUS ONLY ON LOVING THOUGHTS.

How and when to recite this mantra: Recite this mantra three times quietly to yourself as you are drifting off to sleep.

How this mantra can help you: As we begin winding down for the day, it is common to start feeling anxieties and stresses that were skimmed over during the day. Often it is only when our minds are still that we begin to tune into some of the deeper emotions that are lingering within, and sometimes this can bring up worries and doubts we didn't even know we had! This mantra is designed to get you focusing on only the loving thoughts that float in and out of your mind as you prepare to drift off to sleep. Even if you feel heavy emotions arising, try finding the love and try viewing things from a place of compassion. This mantra serves as a reminder to be kind, loving, and compassionate with yourself, especially as you drift off into sleep. This mantra also serves as a reminder to think lovingly about your life and to feel grateful for and proud of all the things you accomplished and achieved. By focusing on loving thoughts, your mind can relax and experience a deep and restful night of sleep.

INDEX